Galveston
LORE, LEGEND, AND DOWNRIGHT LIES

Galveston

LORE, LEGEND, AND DOWNRIGHT LIES

Gini Fendler-Brown

AND

Max Rizley, Jr.

EAKIN PRESS  Austin, Texas

FIRST EDITION
Copyright © 2000
By Gini Fendler-Brown and Max Rizley, Jr.
Published in the United States of America
By Eakin Press
A Division of Sunbelt Media, Inc.
P.O. Drawer 90159 ⏏ Austin, Texas 78709-0159
email: eakinpub@sig.net
💻 website: www.eakinpress.com 💻
ALL RIGHTS RESERVED.
1   2   3   4   5   6   7   8   9
1-57168-441-7

Cover photo by Robert John Mihovil, who served as
Director of Photographic illustrations

Library of Congress Cataloging-in-Publication Data

Fendler-Brown, Gini
Galveston: Lore, Legend, and Downright Lies / by Gini Fendler-Brown and Max
Rizley, Jr.–1st ed.
p.   cm.
Includes bibliographical references.
ISBN 1-57168-441-7 (pbk.)
1. Galveston (Tex.)–History–Anecdotes. 2. Galveston (Tex.)–Folklore. 3. Galveston
Island (Tex.)–History–Anecdotes. 4. Galveston Island (Tex.)–Folklore. I. Rizley, Max
II. Title.

F394.G@ F36 2000
976.4'139–dc21   00-047649

Dedicated to the memory of Maury Darst: historian, journalist, teacher, friend, and a fount of Galveston lore and legend—but not one downright lie.

CONTENTS

Acknowledgments ix
Foreword xi
Introduction xiii
Prologue: "And The Band Played On!" xv

Part I: Land, Sea, and Sky

From Snakes, 'Gators, to Geese—
  Man and Animal Share an Island of Sand 3
Galveston: A Bird's-Eye Perspective 5
Isle Fog Has a Mind of Its Own 8
Through Storm, Fire, Famine, and War,
  the Oleander City Keeps Blooming 11
Winter on the Isle: Not So Cold, But 15
The Bolivar Ferry:
  Who Says You Can't Get Somethin' for Nothin'? 17

Part II: Rich Man, Poor Man, Indian Chief

The Karankawas: Ultimate B.O.I.s 23
Germans' Stamp on Galveston
  Lives on at Garten Verein 26
To Know Galveston, Know the East Enders. 28
Nicholas J. Clayton:
  Dreams and Doodles in Brick and Mortar 31
Henry Rosenberg Quenched
  More Than the Thirst for Knowledge. 35
LeRoy Columbo Never Heard a Cry for Help—
  But He Answered Nearly 1,000 of Them 36
Charlie Bertolino: Father, Fisherman, Friend to All 39

You Don't Cuss at Sonny's Place . . .
   and You Don't Shoot at Junior!. 42
To Savvas and Katina—
   Whose Grasp Exceeded Their Dreams 44
Two Mayors, One Island, and a Wealth of History 47
Some are Islanders, Some Just Live Here 50

Part III: Blood, Sweat, and Tears

Ashton Villa: Grande Dame of
   Galveston's "Broadway Beauties" 55
Isle's "Old Lady"
   Made as Much History as She Reported 57
Isle's Heart Beats in Historic Neighborhoods 60
The 1900 Storm:
   A Shattered City, a Strengthened People. 62
The Seawall: Robert's Rule for Nature 66
Islanders Won Their Home
   Back from the Sea in Grade-Raising. 69
The 1880s: Birth of the Beachfront 71
From Parading Butchers to Splash Day,
   Islanders Love a Party 77
The Bay Froze, the Snow Drifted,
   but Isle Streetcars Rolled On 80
Auto's Advent Rattled Isle into Twentieth Century 82
Isle Aviation Takes Off
   with New Airport, "Wrong-Way" Corrigan 84
Of Nickel Ice Cream, Soda Fizzes,
   and Warm Isle Evenings. 87
Wartime: Soldiers, Sweethearts, Carousels
   and Moonlit Beaches 89
Galveston's Summer of '42:
   Lonely GIs Ashore, U-Boats Offshore. 92
When People Rode Trains,
   They Rode Them to Galveston. 94
Even Strong Hearts Got Weak-Kneed
   on the Mountain Speedway 96
1958: Slow Dancing at the Marine Room,
   Utah Carl on the Motorola. 99

Tropic Isle Proves Poor Retirement Home
  for Geriatric Lobster. 101
UTMB: Tomorrow's Doctors Bloom Today
  in the Oleander City. 104
Grand Opera House's Rescue
  Saves More Than a Theater 106
The Strand: "The More Things Change . . ."   109

Part IV: Lore, Legend, and Downright Lies

Friends, Romans . . . Galvestonians?. 115
Jean Lafitte: The Heart of a Legend. 117
Bolivar Watermelon Man Last of Lafitte's Corsairs 121
"Think Snow"—But Carefully!" 126
Galveston's "Golden Age":
  Burning the Candle at Both Ends. 128
From "Love by the Ton" to Mortified Church Ladies,
  Postoffice Street Has Seen It All 131
Isolated Beaches Drew More Than Beachcombers
  During Prohibition Era. 135
World War II: Sailors, Sheep, and Swine
  Kept Pelican Island Safe for Democracy 138
Semper Fi: Isle Marines March Off to War—and Rivalry. . . 140
The *City of Galveston* Flies Off to War 142
Texas Tradition Takes a Twist
  with Bolivar Goat Roundup 144
Galveston's Ghosts:
  How Many "D.O.I.s" Haunt Isle Nights?. 147
Demolition Banishes More Than Just Old Buildings 150

Epilogue: Today, Tomorrow, and Always

With Dreams of the Future in Our Heads 155
And So, to Bed. 159
More Lore, Historical Resources. 163

ACKNOWLEDGMENTS

Where do I start to thank the many, many people whose tales and anecdotes wound up in our Tuesday-evening storytimes, and, ultimately, here?

I am indebted to the writers of numerous articles about Galveston from which I gleaned bits and pieces of stories about Isle life: Steve Long, Frances Kay Harris, Steve Mayo, Maury Darst, Harold Scarlett, Joel Kirkpatrick, Kim Franklin, Pep Valdes, Herman L. Koester, Mabel Hempel, Jim Brigance, and especially my co-author, Max Rizley, Jr.

Many B.O.I.s shared their memories with me, even though I was not one of them but a "Yankee immigrant," and I want to thank them for their friendship and confidence: Ruby Bertolino, Mrs. John Miranda, the members of the Jean Lafitte Society, George Mitchell, Robert Mihovil, Jeanne Kunz Janota, and Eddie Hunter.

In the early days of compiling this work, Harry and Kim contributed immeasurably. As the years passed, the encouragement of Tina, Jack, Kathryn, Ann, Hac, Barbara, Annette, Brenda, Frank, Hazel, Angie, Elaine, Maxine, Betty, Joanne, Jeanne, Ian, Palmer, Susan, Jennifer, Roberta, Joan, and, never to be forgotten, those who attended the summer band concerts and offered applause, additions, corrections, and suggestions for future stories. These stories belong to all of us.

I read, learned from, and drew upon this partial list of books and authors to whom I owe a debt of gratitude: *Galveston: A History of the Island,* by Gary Cartwright; *Galveston: A History,* by David G. McComb; *Ray Miller's Galveston,* by Ray Miller; *Pioneers of West Galveston Island,* by Roberta Marie Christensen; *Bob's*

Reader, by Bob Nesbitt; *The Galveston Era,* by Earl Wesley Fornell; *Texas, American Guide Series,* by the Texas State Highway Commission; *History of the Confederate Navy,* by J. Thomas Sharf; *They Made Their Own Law,* by Melanie Wiggins; *Commodore Moore and the Texas Navy,* by Tom Henderson Wells; *Treasures of Galveston Bay,* by Carroll Lewis; *Custodians of the Coast,* by Lynn M. Alpern; *Letters from Sandy and Recalled Recollections,* by I. H. Kempner; *Oleander Odyssey,* by Harold M. Hyman; *Odd Texas,* by Jack Harper and John Newbern; *The Indians of Texas,* by W. W. Newcomb, Jr.; *The Wartime Journals of Charles Lindbergh,* by Charles Lindbergh.

Invaluable information was provided by *The Galveston Daily News, InBetween Magazine, The Houston Post, The Houston Chronicle,* and *The Dallas Morning News.*

To Casey Green, Shelly Kelly, and Anna Peebler at the Rosenberg Library, my heartfelt thanks for patiently helping me for more than ten years.

A special thank you to Melanie Wiggins for her guidance and encouragement and to Tanya Baker's Key Designs, whose computer talents were remarkable and indispensable.

What I have just done is the riskiest thing I have ever done—because I am certain I have overlooked someone, and to them, my profoundest apologies. I still love you all.

Gini Fendler-Brown
July 2000

FOREWORD

By Jan Coggeshall
Galveston Mayor 1984–1989

The seventy-second annual Fourth of July Summer Band Concert was presented in 2000 at the Sealy Gazebo with probably all the enthusiasm of the first celebration. Held in conjunction with the Galveston Beach Band's weekly Tuesday-night concerts, flags were waving and patriotic music was led by band director Frank Incaprera, Jr., continuing a tradition observed by seven generations of Galvestonians. Amid the brass band's rousing marches and show tunes, Gini Brown presented one of her weekly vignettes of Galveston history, many of which are presented in this book. She has delighted her Tuesday-evening audiences with stories of events from our Island's past or of Galveston's famous "characters."

Facts, fables, and foibles are braided like a rope into the lore of our barrier island, where physical destruction, reconstruction, and ongoing renewal have created a broad canvas for Gini's weekly sojourns into our past.

Held for many years in Menard Park on the Seawall, the concerts moved to the Mary Moody Northen Plaza, owned by Rosenberg Library, in the 1980s. A permanent gazebo, designed by David Oliver, was donated by the children of George and Eugenia Sealy and constructed on the site behind Ashton Villa and in front of the library. The City of Galveston agreed to maintain the gazebo, and subsequent city councils continued to fund the summer concerts from the annual city budget, under a permissive clause in the city charter. Area band directors and local musicians make up a significant element of the performances, and they return year after year.

Every week, telling her stories, Gini Brown looks out over a crowd of children anxiously awaiting the weekly children's flag parade, as park benches and folding chairs fill with Island residents as well as visitors from around the county, state, and the world. Frank Incaprera, Jr., always wanders through the crowds, asking visitors where they are from. Each week, local guest entertainers perform, and a Galveston Senior Night closes the season every August.

One of the most-senior nights occurred in 1991, when Frank Incaprera, Sr., at age 100, conducted some of the music he had written, including the "Oleander City March." With his wife in attendance for the birthday celebration, Frank Senior had conducted all or part of the concerts for over sixty years. Frank Junior, a retired U.S. Army Corps of Engineers economist, took over the reins of the band in 1962.

After you've read this book, come join Gini and other visitors for the free Tuesday-night concerts every summer, and bring the kids and grandchildren for a never-to-be-forgotten evening.

Children gather at the George and Eugenia Sealy Gazebo for their weekly summer flag parade.

—Robert John Mihovil

INTRODUCTION

When the legend becomes fact—print the legend.
—Edmond O'Brien in *The Man Who Shot Liberty Valance*

This is not a history of Galveston Island, for history is written by historians, fine people with lengthy academic pedigrees and curricula vitae instead of résumés. If you seek hard data on the Who, What, When, Where, Why, and How in the life and times of the Isle, then put this book back on the shelf.

Our working title was "Tuesday Night Love Letters: An Affair with Galveston Island," in reference to Isle "History Lady" Gini Brown's five-minute storytimes during the Galveston Beach Band's summer performances in the pavilion behind Ashton Villa. Gini's "love letters" celebrate the nonhistorical history of the Island, the "little" stories of people and events—the legends, the gossip, the "didja hears"—shared by local folk over back-alley fences, between doughnut-shop stools, around cafeteria tables, at church socials and family reunions.

But we've also included, as a sort of *mise en scène,* some pieces intended to help set a mood, to provide verbal lighting and staging for Gini's tales of these unique people and their unique stories.

"Galveston Island, off Texas"—as many who live here pointedly refer to it—is a unique place, so different in pace, culture, worldview, and even speech patterns from the rest of the state it (often begrudgingly) is a part of, that the mile or so of bay that separates it from the mainland often seems like an ocean. The "other" Texas grew up in boundless stretches of prairie, mountain, and desert, and its story is a dry-land tale of cattle kings, oil barons, dust storms, and climates arctic to torrid.

Galveston is a creature of boundaries, a sandy cowlick surrounded by bay and ocean. Its tale is a sea story, roughed out in as many tongues and cultures as the restless Gulf could toss up on its shores, edited by close quarters and shared hardships. The other Texas brags about moving on, spreading out, pushing the frontier endlessly westward; Galvestonians' pride is rooted in building a bustling city and a gracious lifestyle within the tight confines of a Gulf Coast barrier island. The other Texas once had to contend with Indian raids and border disputes, bloody struggles that now reside in the past; Galvestonians have had to ride out Nature's most determined efforts to destroy them—an unceasing battle that will never be retired into the pages of history.

Here, then, are the stories of Galveston as Galvestonians know them: The names, events, and snippets of everyday life, the collective story of an island people. It is their lore, their legends, even a few downright lies: Galvestonians' history as it should be—no matter what some scholar across the Causeway says.

Max Rizley, Jr.
July 2000

PROLOGUE

"And The Band Played On!"

Galvestonians know it is summertime on the Island when the sky turns a silky, soft blue and the warm, sweet oleander perfume rides a gentle Gulf breeze. You can almost taste the sea salt in the air; the sunsets are salmon-hued, streaked with gold and mauve. The ocean softly kisses the sand, and the sound of music fills the summer evening.

More than one hundred years ago, in 1883, the Beach Hotel was the focal point for Galveston social activity. Brass bands played six nights a week on the lawn of this, the only hotel on the beach. Rousing marches and romantic symphonic music entertained whole families. Children played on the beach . . . young lovers strolled at the water's edge . . . music lovers gathered in chairs on the lawn.

Beginning in 1897, Wednesday-night concerts at the Garten Verein, the German dancing pavilion that stands to this day in Kempner Park, started another Galveston tradition. "On summer evenings young people danced and kindled romances," wrote Gary Cartwright in his book *Galveston, A History of the Island*. "German waiters served platters of cold meat, lemonade, and steins of beer. Membership was limited to 500 and women were forbidden to smoke or use rouge or lipstick."

The popularity of bands increased, and at one time there were seven or more summer bands playing on the Island. In the early 1920s, a group of musicians sponsored by the Beach Association—among them Frank Incaprera, a handsome young gent from Cefalu, Sicily—gathered together and played in different places at irregular times. The concerts became so popular that in 1928 the citizens voted to allocate one mill—one-tenth of a cent—per $100 to support a Galveston Municipal Band so that the concerts would always be free and open for everyone.

And so they have been, and continue to be, even as the tradition of outdoor band music on the Isle approaches a third century. Today, it is still Frank Incaprera—son of the Frank Incaprera who joined the band as young man in the 1920s—and his Galveston Beach Band who keep this rare musical heritage alive and well on summer Tuesday evenings at the Mary Moody Northen Pavilion, on Sealy Street just behind Ashton Villa.

As the shadows lengthen and the midsummer heat slowly relinquishes its grip, the people gather. Children chase each other up and down the rows of wooden benches facing the stage and clamber over the abstract metal sculptures that dot the plaza's grassy margins. Vendors sell ice cream and cold drinks, and if it's election season the politicians buzz around like mosquitoes, shaking hands and handing out cards and fans touting their qualifications for office. Friends greet friends . . . lawn chairs are carefully placed and unfolded, coolers opened . . . the best bench seats are staked out. Band members arrive and prepare for the evening's selections, running a scale here, a snatch of a Sousa march there.

Then, suddenly, it is time. Frank Incaprera steps into the gazebo and takes up his baton . . . the buzzing crowd grows quiet . . . and with an emphatic downbeat, the musicians launch into "If My Friends Could See Me Now." The baton waves, dips, soars, and points; it stabs the air, drawing a flourish from the trumpets, a brisk "ta-ra-ra" from the trombones, an exclamation point from the drums—and, finally, a warm wave of applause from the audience.

Halfway through the concert, with horns muted, the strains of "Ebb Tide" softly fill the air. The musicians put their instruments down. From amid the crowd at stage left, a petite woman with a twinkle in her eye and a sheaf of paper in her hands strides across the plaza and stops front and center, and the audience leans forward in anticipation.

It's time for the "History Lady" to take the stage.

Alias Gini Fendler-Brown, the History Lady has been sharing her engaging tales about the people, the history, and the legends that are Galveston Island with Beach Band audiences since 1989. To call them "history lessons" would be much too dry a description of what the History Lady does; rather, her five-minute conversations are fond recollections of the people and events that give this island city its unique character.

Part history, part folklore (with a hearty dash of gossip, the national sport of Galveston Island), Gini Brown's little "Tuesday Night love letters" are as much a part of Galveston's character as seagulls, oleanders, Gulf storms, West Bay sunsets—and, of course, the History Lady herself.

So grab a seat, buy a Coke, and don't forget to take an American flag from the young man who is passing them out— you'll need it for the kids' flag parade. Relax as the sunset sea breeze raises its cooling benediction to another sweltering summer's day, and indulge in that wonderfully Norman Rockwellian institution, the "brass band concert in the park," something most other cities today can only dream about, and envy. Judging from the number of young families that bring lawn chairs and blankets and babies and make an evening of it, the band will play on well into tomorrow, under its golden canopy of Galveston's summer sunsets.

But hush! Here comes the History Lady . . .

PART I
Land, Sea, and Sky

From Snakes, 'Gators, to Geese—Man and Animal Share an Island of Sand

Our sunny sandbar is truly an island of sand. In 1891 a team of water-well drillers bored 1,500 feet deep and found no underlying bedrock. Nonetheless, our island has been here nigh onto 180 million years—still, relatively recent in geological terms.

Of course, we have lots of wonderful water all around us. And yes, we have miles and miles of beautiful beaches, and creatures of the wild, and fish, and seabirds—even snakes and the occasional alligator.

At one time, the Karankawa Indians referred to this land as Snake Island. Snakes, while plentiful in the marshes and dunes, are rarely seen in town—"rarely," that is, not "never." Joel Kirkpatrick, longtime Isle journalist, tells the tale of Willie Burns, who was our police chief in 1964. He was "resting at home while his wife was working in her garden. He heard her scream, 'Willie, it's a rattlesnake! Don't move! Call the police!' There was a five-foot rattler on the sidewalk. 'Call the police?' he asked. 'Why should I call the police? I'm the Chief of Police!' And with that pronouncement, he killed the snake with a rake."

We all know we can catch and enjoy a meal of crab, oysters, flounder, and redfish. More interesting, perhaps, are the ducks—especially to a hunter. Kirkpatrick, also a duck hunter, wrote:

"Well, every morning during the duck and goose hunting sea-

3

". . . even the occasional alligator." This one was captured at 99th Street and Stewart Road.
—Robert John Mihovil

son, the sun brings the daylight, and sometimes it smears a salmon-colored sunrise along the horizon. The wind frosts over the ponds with ripples and leaves its footprints on the marsh-grass, and hunters crouch in blinds and look and listen for wild-fowl, and breathe the fertile air of marshlands. And finally, ducks come, wings whistling and cupped feet lowered, into the decoys, and they're too beautiful to shoot—almost."

In this prime hunting area, the hunters, like the fishermen, enjoy telling their tall tales. Kirkpatrick recounts this one:

A hunter was bragging in a local cafe, "Why, with one shot I killed twenty-five ducks."

A stranger got up from a table, walked over and looked him in the eye and asked, "Do you know who I am?"

"No."

"Well, I'm the new game warden, and what you did is illegal."

The hunter paused and then said, "Do you know who I am?"

"No," the warden replied.

"I'm the biggest liar in town!"

Then, there is the story of a hunter who flagged down the manager of a game preserve during the season and said, "I've shot some geese I can't identify. Can you help?"

"Sure," replied the manager as the hunter opened his trunk. He looked in at a pair of white birds and laughed. "Why man, you've shot seagulls!"

The huntsman turned red and angrily retorted, "You can't fool me! These are geese! I live in Galveston and I ought to know what seagulls look like!" He slammed the trunk and left.

The manager could only wonder what the seagulls tasted like at the hunter's table.

Galveston: A Bird's-Eye Perspective

Did you know that some two thousand bird watchers visit us each year, since our island is on a migratory flyway? Indeed, Galveston is more than just a brief stopover along that flyway, it is a vital landfall to thousands of exhausted birds seeking rest and food after a grueling flight over thousands of miles of open ocean—or a last chance to fill up on high-energy foods before beginning that marathon leg of their yearly journey.

At Galveston Island State Park, a two-thousand-acre preserve that includes wetlands, salt meadows, beaches, dunes, and coastal prairie, the migratory birds include cuckoos, thrushes, orioles, warblers, tanagers, buntings, and grosbeaks. In 1962 an "extinct" Eskimo curlew was spotted and photographed. Permanent residents include the mockingbird, great blue heron,

Seagulls—good swimmers, poor walkers.
—Robert John Mihovil

snowy egret, white ibis, mottled duck, bobwhite quail, mourning dove, red-bellied woodpecker, starling, red-winged blackbird, house sparrow, seaside sparrow, marsh wren, meadowlark, and horned lark, as well as the usual coastal birds such as sandpipers, gulls, plovers, rails, terns, and pelicans.

The white pelican, a freshwater migratory bird that winters in Galveston, has not had the trouble of the brown pelican, which lives here on a year-round basis. The browns were plentiful as late as 1955, when flocks of fifty to sixty at a time could be seen floating on the water. But they proved to be sensitive to DDT, and after 1960 the brown pelican population went into a severe decline. Now an endangered species, they are making a strong comeback here. You'll see them soaring over the blue Gulf waters—sometimes just barely above the waves—then, spiraling high, they take aim and dive straight into the water for food. They nest on the shores of Offatt's Bayou, where you can see them just around sunrise and again at sunset.

Much hardier are the seagulls; there are fifty-three species in Galveston. They are graceful, buoyant fliers, good swimmers, and poor walkers. Most gulls are scavengers and act like beach bums. They hover and pick up morsels wherever they can—everything from dead fish to discarded French fries. They are the sanitation crew of the beach. The most common variety is the laughing gull, noted for its dark red legs, thirty-two-inch wingspan, and, of course, its raucous, braying laugh. It lives for eight to fifteen years. There is also the Franklin gull, with black head and black wing tips. The herring gull has a fifty-four-inch wingspan and migrates to the south for the winter, and the ring-billed gull sports yellow legs, a forty-eight-inch wingspan, and a black ring on its bill.

Terns also share the beach with the gulls. The terns have narrower wings than the gulls, and, like the pelicans, they cruise the waves, dive into the water, and live off fresh fish. One variety, the arctic tern, is a yearly visitor; this vagabond holds the world's record for migration—26,000 miles round trip—from the high Arctic, south to Antarctica, and back again, every year.

Just how the many species of birds that call at Galveston during their fall and spring migrations navigate over such long distances is one of Nature's mysteries. Some speculate that they can hear the booming of far-off surf and keep that sound on one side or the other to plot their course. Others have proposed that microscopic deposits of iron in the birds' brains act as internal compasses, allowing them to track the earth's magnetic field.

Whatever the mechanism for their amazing feats of global navigation, it is obvious our avian friends are closely attuned to the natural rhythms of this old Planet Earth, and many people claim to "read" their habits as harbingers of natural events to come. For example, it is said that when the gulls fly in high, spi-raling circles over the city, it is a warning of stormy weather.

But I don't think that's always true—I have often seen my gull friends climbing high above me into dazzling, clear skies, work-ing the updrafts as the clouds break apart—gliding in lazy cir-cles, wings motionless, as the shifting air currents lift and then drop them in the summer sky, high over the sun-splashed panorama of land and sea that is our own Galveston Island.

Isle Fog Has a Mind of Its Own

AN ESSAY BY MAX RIZLEY, JR.

A FOGGY DAY—We really do have some pea-soupers around here, don't we? A gambling ship found that out the hard way three days after Christmas some years ago, when a socked-in channel turned an evening's cruise into a fifteen-hour, seagoing slumber party for its 700 passengers.

I'd've thought the ship's operators would have had more of a plan for foggy weather when they decided to make Galveston their home port; after all, our wintertime fogs certainly aren't any secret.

You know, fog is a strange creature, more living organism than mere meteorology. Fog has a mind of its own, and a crafty one at that. Fog doesn't spring up just anywhere. Oh, no—it lies in wait for its victims, hiding just over the horizon or around the next headland. It waits until the hapless mariner is as far from safe har-bor as he can possibly get—and only then does it make its move.

It lays its plans carefully, feeling out its prey, getting to know just who it is dealing with.

If you're a lubber out there—perhaps you're just getting the feel of the brand-new aluminium skiff you got for Christmas — the fog sneaks up, coming in a wisp at a time, building slowly, slowly, so slowly that you don't realize what's happening until you're already engulfed in a cottony mantle.

Ah, but if the fog senses that you're an old salt, wise to the ways

Galveston's Tall Ship Elissa *sails up the ship channel in an early-morning winter fog.*

—Robert John Mihovil

of wind and tide, it pounces, bulling out from its hiding place like a roiling cloud of smoke, taking you by simple speed, rather than by cunning. You can't outrun it, even when you see it coming.

And once it has you in its grip, the fog plays eerie tricks. Most people think of fog as merely an obscuring curtain, but it is far, far more than that.

Fog is a ventriloquist, for one thing. There you sit in your little twenty-foot sloop, swallowed up in snowy whiteness, afraid to move—and you hear, to your horror, the deep-throated *moo* of a ship's whistle. A BIG ship's whistle. Coming closer. Is it—where? Ah—in front . . . no, wait, it's off to starboard . . . no, no . . . over there? It seems to be everywhere!

The hair stands up on the back of your neck as your inner ear picks up the subtle pressure of something big and heavy approaching. You hear the heart-stopping hiss of a massive bow knifing through the still water—nearby—unseen—then the fog parts in a dramatic swirl and a rusty steel mountain emerges, just off your port bow, sliding past so close by you can count the welds in the hull.

You hear, briefly, somewhere in the murk above, the crackle of a radio and perhaps a quick rudder order; maybe you catch a glimpse of a face at a porthole, feel the heat of boiler fires somewhere in the bowels of this steel Gibraltar—and then it's gone, just like that, the ponderous *splush-splush-splush* of a prop fading away into the mists, leaving you quite alone again in the fog, just you and your pounding heart.

Then the fog, having had its little joke for the day, suddenly lifts, the all-enveloping blindness replaced in an instant with a glorious vista of sea and land and sun and sky—there, a mile downchannel, is the freighter that almost sent you to the bottom.

And as you shake out your canvas for the hurried trip home, you pause a moment, puzzled, as you hear—no, it couldn't be, could it?—a low chuckle, seeming to come from everywhere and nowhere at once.

Through Storm, Fire, Famine, and War, the Oleander City Keeps Blooming

Well, we made it! The city of Galveston has survived wars, storms, fires, and hard times since we were chartered in 1839. We've come a long way since that first hardy band of pioneers settled on this barrier island in the Gulf of Mexico. And something else has grown right along with us, something that is as much a part of Galveston Island as its beaches and seagulls: A beautiful plant, the oleander—and because of it, we are known as the "Oleander City" . . . or should I say, the Oleander Island?

In the late spring, before the blast-furnace heat of summer sets in, the Isle is fairly aglow with the multi-hued blaze of thousands of blooming oleander bushes—in yards, in parks, along the freeway medians and down the tree-shaded esplanades of our major avenues. They bloom white, red, maroon, pink, cream-colored, and every shade in between; some scent the air with a gentle, sweet perfume, while others make up with brilliant color what they lack in fragrance.

To see so many oleanders flourishing in one place, you might be surprised to find out that the shrub is not a native Islander.

The oleander apparently originated in the Mediterranean area, and in Israel it still grows naturally in the Golan Heights and Upper Galilee. In 1841 Joseph Osterman brought oleander plants to Galveston from Jamaica in tubs aboard his trading schooner. His sister, Mrs. Isadore Dyer, lived on the Island, and he gave them to her. She shared cuttings with her friends, and this led to the most extensive collection of oleanders to be found anywhere in the world. Mrs. Dyer lived at 25th and Sealy; if you go there, you will see a bronze plaque designating an oleander growing there as being from the original plant Joseph Osterman brought to the Isle—a fragrant double-pink variety. Many Galvestonians, in fact, have inherited plants that are from 75 to more than 100 years old.

During the 1800s in Galveston, when ladies dressed to attend social functions, they would wear clusters of fresh oleander blossoms. A gift of oleander flowers was a sentimental gesture.

In Galveston, long known as the "Oleander City," the gift of a cluster of fresh blooms is still considered an expression of loving and sentimental thoughts.

—Robert John Mihovil

Almost all homes had container-grown oleander plants; in the summer the oleanders were planted in gardens, and in the winter, put in tubs and sheltered. Today, many of the plants on the Island are left in the ground year round. Although a bad freeze will kill the leaves and branches—as happened in the notorious Christmas freeze of 1989—they are a hardy shrub, and after pruning they will soon return to their original beauty.

George Sealy, Jr., a member of one of Galveston's early families, followed the interest of other relatives and devoted years and considerable money to the beautification of Galveston. His great interest, and the support of Eddie Barr, father of County Commissioner Eddie Barr, resulted in the development and propagation of over sixty different varieties of oleanders. During World War II, they shipped over 600,000 plants throughout the United States and Canada and gave free plants to servicemen stationed at Fort Crockett, to visitors to the Island, and to hundreds of Galvestonians. Plants were sent to President Roosevelt, the Duchess of Windsor, and many others, to promote Galveston.

Gee, what a nice precedent to set! Why don't we give oleanders to newly elected presidents, or to visiting heads of state, as a goodwill gift from the Oleander City on Texas' Golden Gulf Coast?

Reaching from the beach into the Gulf of Mexico, rock groins show a rare touch of winter's icy fingers. Crystal icicles sparkle in the early morning sun . . . but only for a brief time.

— Robert John Mihovil

Winter on the Isle: Not So Cold, But . . .

AN ESSAY BY MAX RIZLEY, JR.

Bang.

Bang . . . Bang . . . Bang, bang, bang . . . Bang.

The first fall norther whistled through here tonight, and that loose plank on the patio fence is banging fitfully in the chilly wind.

Bang. Bang.

It's a sad sound, a lonesome sound, a funeral bell tolling the passing of summer.

I love this little island dearly, but it is the most depressing place when winter comes. I think that's because Galveston is designed, built, and colored for a tropical clime; somehow, our lighthearted roses and teals and peaches and yellows don't have the same cheery glow under winter's sodden gray skies that they do under a smiling summer's sun.

The wind whistles cruelly through the chinks and gaps in our lightly built tropic walls and rattles the desiccated fronds on the palm trees like skeleton fingers in the night. The generous double-hung windows that admit summer's refreshing Gulf breezes are scarcely competition for winter's bitter northerly blast.

Bang. Bang. Bang, bang.

Even my beloved Gulf puts on a somber winter face, turning muddy and ugly, growling against the rock groins and throwing up despairing plumes of spindrift as its waves struggle beachward against contrary winds.

Yes, we have been cheated here on the Texas coast when it comes to winter. We get all the flus and frozen plants and busted pipes, and none of the paybacks winter gives the folks in colder latitudes. Farther north, and not all that much farther, the northers that bring the frigid temperatures also bring the snow, which covers the brown grass and naked trees with its magical white mantle. And the storms, although fiercer in intensity, tend to whistle right on through, leaving the sparkling white landscape bathed in the year's most brilliant sunshine.

Here, of course, the fronts always run out of gas just offshore and sit there for weeks on end, keeping us under that dreary, damp pall. And it never snows; only when the weather's blown on through and the sky's cleared out does it get cold enough to snow—which it can't, not from such dazzlingly brilliant, ice-blue skies.

Bang.

Like I said, I love this little sandbar dearly and wouldn't leave it for the world. But when it gets gray and wet and everything smells like the refineries upwind, I can't help remembering my childhood, in a more northerly spot, when I'd lie abed and listen to that special hissing sound on the roof—not at all like falling rain—and look out the window to see the big, fat flakes dancing in the cone of light under the streetlamp outside, then snuggle down under the covers to dream of sleds and snowmen.

But then, of course, I remember that back in those days— along about April, when I was still slipping on patches of ice lingering in the shady places—I used to envy the folks who lived in tropical climes, where winter wasn't such a long and drawn-out affair. "Come March," I'd tell myself, "I'll be in T-shirts and shorts . . ."

Bang. Bang. BANG!

" . . . out in the yard, fixing that dad-blamed fence!"

The Bolivar Ferry: Who Says You Can't Get Somethin' for Nothin'?

Have you been on a ferryboat ride lately?

Well, naturally, because we're an island, we have a wonderful ferry ride. The Galveston–Bolivar ferry, linking the Isle with the Bolivar Peninsula, has been an important link to the Texas mainland since the early 1900s. Today, the ferry is operated free to the public by the Texas Department of Transportation, through funds generated by the state gasoline tax.

The state has operated the ferry since 1933, when it acquired the facility from private operators. Back then, cars and trailers were charged 25 cents, and six-wheel trucks, 50 cents. (I wonder what they would have charged one of today's eighteen-wheelers?) Pedestrians rode the ferries for free—at a time when, ashore, bus fares were 7 cents for adults and 4 cents for kids. The schedule was six daily roundtrips, during daylight hours only. Today, the ferries run twenty-four hours a day, and a holiday weekend will see about ninety roundtrips.

The steel-hulled motor-ferry vessels make the thirteen-minute trip at about 12 knots and handle almost two million vehicles and over five-and-a-half million people every year. The 600- to 1,100-gross-ton ferryboats carry a crew of six. With two 865-horsepower propulsion motors and a twenty-by-fifty-foot passenger lounge on the top deck, they cost from $600,000 to just over $8 million. Two boats were built at Todd Shipyards in Galveston, one in Port Arthur, one in Indiana, one in Mobile, Alabama, and one in Escatawpa, Mississippi. The bright red, blue, green, and yellow-trimmed vessels are a colorful sight as they traverse the gray-blue waters of Bolivar Roads under a clear blue Texas sky.

Take a ferry ride from Galveston's East End to Bolivar Peninsula. You'll surely discover unequaled delight. Go early and see the golden, midmorning water, with its dancing patches of sunlight and shade. Breathe in those cool, fresh Gulf breezes. Listen to the raucous cry of seagulls as they soar over the back of the ferry, asking for a handout (so don't forget to bring stale bread or crackers to feed them). Standing at the front of the boat, you'll probably see the playful bottle-nosed dolphins, and if you are lucky they will be playing close to the bow in the waves as the ferry slices through the water.

Look for majestic pelicans as they glide low over the water or perhaps just float lazily on the midchannel chop as the current carries them along. You'll pass picturesque shrimp boats, a yacht harbor picketed by row upon row of sailboat masts—and heading up the ship channel, the lumbering tankers loom large on the horizon. The close-by passage of ocean-going steamships and cruise liners adds excitement to the trip.

Traveling to Galveston from Bolivar in the evening, you'll watch the most spectacular sunset in the world, all salmon-pink and gold and crimson, mirrored in the brooding, dark, evening face of Bolivar Roads.

The Bolivar ferry ride—one of Galveston's most unpublicized, yet most fascinating, attractions. And it's all free!

The ferryboat Gibb Gilchrist, *the connection between Galveston Island and the Bolivar Peninsula, glides into the landing slip.*

—Robert John Mihovil

PART II

Rich Man, Poor Man, Indian Chief

The Karankawas: Ultimate B.O.I.s

B.O.I.: Abbreviation for "Born on the Island." Ultimate distinction for a Galvestonian, second only to having survived, or having relatives who survived, the 1900 Storm.

More than five hundred years ago, there were many Indian tribes in southern Texas. One tribe, which inhabited what we now call Galveston Island, was known by some as "people who walk in water." But the tribe chose its own name, one that came from two Indian words: *karan* ("dog") and *kawa* ("to love"). Since the tribe traveled with small, barkless, fox-like dogs, they became known as the "dog lovers," and we know them by this name, too—Karankawas.

Although the Karankawas were virtually extinct by the time Texas became a republic, no tribe in the state archives is more maligned. According to Gary Cartwright, one author writes the Karankawas off as "the meanest, greediest, laziest, most treacherous, lecherous, vicious, cowardly, insolent aborigines of the Southwest."

But anthropological evidence, as well as the accounts of those who encountered them, paints a very different picture of these Galveston Indians.

The Karankawas were a physically imposing race, very tall, strongly built and magnificently formed, with slender hands and feet. They were not very dark, and many of them had delicate features and, without exception, splendid teeth. Their coarse

23

This bust of a Karankawa Indian woman was created by Betty Pat Gatliff, an internationally recognized teacher of forensic sculpture and a retired medical illustrator. The Columella beads on the Karankawa woman's necklace were made from the center spines of conch shells. The beads were found in the Indian burial grounds.

—Photo by Betty Pat Gatliff, courtesy the Houston Museum of Natural Science

hair, bleached cinnamon red by the sun, hung to the waist and was frequently braided and often secured by rattles from a snake.

The men wore breechcloths and the women, flimsy skirts of Spanish moss. Children wore no clothing until they were ten years old, and the maidens of the tribe wore modest deerhide skirts. Untanned deerhide encircled the wrists of both men and women.

The Karankawas were generous and affectionate, and men were allowed just one wife. They were kind to their children, readily shared their possessions, and observed elaborate marriage and death customs. A study by the Peabody Museum helped to create a profile of the Karankawa people. Shy and cautious, they spoke "with repressed breath which gave a sighing sound to their speech, and they never looked at the person to whom they spoke." The only substantial material possessions treasured by the tribe were their weapons and their canoes—sturdy, twenty-five-foot dugouts that they carved crudely from tree trunks with the bark left on them. The dugouts were their equivalent of the frontiersman's horse. Without them, they could not have survived.

The Karankawas were such skilled archers that they fished with bows and arrows. Like their canoes, these weapons were prized personal possessions. Fashioned from red cedar, the arrows were a yard long and the bows reached from the ground to a man's chin. Although accused of stealing horses and cattle, the truth was they simply could not conceive of anyone owning an animal.

They doted on their children. When a child died, the entire village indulged in ritual wailing that lasted a full year. When a son or brother died, there was more weeping, and members of the dead warrior's household refused to gather food for three months—they lived off provisions unselfishly given by neighbors. And in 1588, when Cabeza de Vaca and his miserable, shipwrecked party washed up and huddled on West Beach, the Karankawas found them, and, understanding their dilemma, sat down and began to weep. They returned each day at sunrise and sunset with food for the marooned party. Cabeza de Vaca recalled: "Verily to see beings so devoid of reason, untutored, so like unto brutes, yet so deeply moved by pity for us . . . ."

Caring and sensitive, crying was as much of part of their culture as saluting or bowing or making the sign of the cross was in Western culture. Their generosity and compassion were unequaled. "Of all the people in the world," Cabeza de Vaca wrote, "they are those who most love their children and treat them best."

Looking back, most hunters coexisted peacefully with the Indians, but treasure seekers and pirates were another breed. As battles increased, the tribe diminished, Cartwright explains. "As their numbers thinned they joined other coastal tribes and slowly retreated into northern Mexico. After 1885 the Karankawas existed no more."

Germans' Stamp on Galveston
Lives On at Garten Verein

"Life in the latter part of the 19th century in Galveston was rich, full and varied," writes David McComb. The flow of immigrants through the port of Galveston provided an abundant mix of cultural societies. More than four thousand crossed the docks each year, mostly headed elsewhere. In the winter, the "newcomers trudged up the middle of the road to the train depot—Russians in fur coats, Swiss in knee britches, Scots with bagpipes, women and children with pots, pans and utensils." Czech farmers headed to the rich black soils of farmlands, and many pitifully poor Norwegian families stopped briefly and moved on.

According to McComb, "The most important group were the Germans, who began their migration before the founding of the city and continued it throughout much of the century. They were a mainly agricultural people, looking to escape European poverty and politics. They influenced Texas culture, and some provided insight about their adopted country."

McComb tells a story culled from the diary of a twenty-year-old German girl who landed in Galveston in 1845 after a trip of forty-four days:

> To her, the town looked like paper toys with houses up on poles ready to be moved one place or another. More impressive, however, was the crowd of German men at the wharf who rushed on board the ship looking for women to marry. She noted a middle-aged baker who spotted a pretty blonde peasant girl and first tried to hire her as a cook. She refused his high wages and said that she was going to her brother, who had paid her travel expenses. Desperate, the baker blurted, "I want to marry you right now!"
>
> The girl coolly replied, "To be married is exactly what I do not want."

Our young diarist wrote that she was pleased with the answer. The first of the independent females had landed.

The Garten Verein, designed by Nicholas Clayton, held Wednesday-night band concerts, which became a Galveston tradition.

—Robert John Mihovil

Gary Cartwright explains that the Germans who remained on the Island, and who made up one-third of the population,

> commissioned celebrated architect Nicholas Clayton to design a dance pavilion, to be called the Garten Verein (Garden Club). . . . Clayton constructed the building as an octagon, with flamboyant verge board, expansive windows, two balustrades, and a cupola, in a sort of a whimsical, "how-dare-the-man" fashion. The mix worked astonishingly well.
>
> The pavilion flew the flags of all nations and was surrounded by a landscaped park with a bowling green, tennis courts and a small zoo. On summer evenings, young people danced and romanced, while red-faced German waiters served platters of cold meat, lemonade, and steins of beer. Wednesday night concerts at the Garten Verein became an Island tradition. Club reg-

ulations were enforced with German thoroughness: membership was limited and maintained at exactly 500, and women were forbidden to smoke or use rouge or lipstick.

"The Wednesday night concerts and picnics have been responsible for more changes of heart in the last twenty years than all the other agencies combined which Cupid has established in Galveston," remarked a reporter in 1897.

McComb tells us that "To honor his parents, Stanley Kempner bought the park in 1923 and presented it as a gift to the city." Although damaged by fire, the Garten Verein was restored and remains a treasure at 27th and Avenue O, where it still hosts picnics, parties, weddings, concerts—and, of course, dances.

To Know Galveston, Know the East Enders

Another summer comes . . . and another . . . and another.

And as the years pass, our island home continues to spread out. One hundred years ago, there was the East End, where almost everyone lived and worked—and the West End, where there were only a few settlers. As time passed, and more and more people jostled for room in this sea-girt city, a "mid-town" inevitably grew up, separating the east and the west.

Now, though, I want to talk about East Enders, with the help of Herman Koester, who married one. Just what—or should I say who—is an East Ender? I've met them, I see them quite often, and they truly have a compelling likability. They are compulsively gregarious and have an inner sense of self-reliance. They have no fear of expressing their opinions on anything or anyone at anytime. East Enders have a strong sense of national pride. They're proud to be Americans, recognizing that this country offers possibilities not available anywhere else, if one works hard and makes the best of one's opportunities. They rarely take themselves too seriously and can always laugh at themselves and at their fellow East Enders. They have a good sense of humor and a great camaraderie.

Homes with tall open windows and long porches were designed to catch the cooling Gulf breezes.

—Robert John Mihovil

They were all born on Galveston Island, from the 1840s to the 1940s, mostly into hard-working immigrant families. At the time, the port of Galveston was the fifth-largest immigration center in the United States, and many of the new arrivals settled right away in Galveston, in its East End. Thus, the area became a melting pot, a cosmopolitan community stretching from 6th Street to 21st Street and from the Bay to the Gulf. Many, it is said, lived their entire lives without setting foot off the Island—after all, Galveston Island was long accessible to the mainland only by one two-lane highway and a ferry. A trip to Houston was a journey that took almost half a day, and when you arrived there was just not too much to see.

They built their homes with high ceilings, large, tall windows, and front porches, to better catch the cooling Gulf breezes. They were also situated no more than a few feet apart—so there were very few secrets in the neighborhood. East Enders realized that everyone had similar faults and problems, which helped them deal rationally with whatever life sent them. No one ever needed a psychiatrist.

Family ties were very close in this era. Grandparents, parents, and children all lived together in their large, old houses, while aunts, uncles, and cousins lived within a block or two. Knowledge, customs, and ideas were handed down from the older to the younger generations. Every evening, the older folks and sometimes the children sat on the large front porches, rocking and watching people walk by. They would stop to talk and gossip, so information quickly spread through the East End. But one had to be careful about whom one spoke, because almost everyone was related to almost everyone else.

Social life was centered around church activities. During the Great Depression, many would be considered as falling below the poverty level, but no one went hungry or demanded food stamps or welfare, as none existed. East Enders were, and are, very self-sufficient and did not need much to survive and thrive.

So it was that on the East End of a small island in the Gulf of Mexico, a unique and admirable breed of human beings evolved. True East Enders, born and bred, are a vanishing breed, and great care should be taken to preserve their heritage, philosophy, and mores. Their presence, their influence, is an essential ingredient in the rich cultural brew that is the very soul of historic Galveston Island.

Nicholas J. Clayton: Dreams and Doodles in Brick and Mortar

On a December morning in 1872, a young Irishman, late of Memphis, Tennessee, arrived on Galveston Island and set out for St. Mary's Cathedral. Passing a pawn shop on Market Street, a ceramic Madonna and Child caught his eye, and he went into the shop and bought it. As though it was an obligation, this young man sought out the local bishop, and during their visit he persuaded the bishop that what the cathedral should have to balance the two towers at the front of the basilica was a center tower. It took the young architect four years to convince the church that the tower should be built. He crowned it with a statue of Mary, Star of the Sea, positioned to look out over the Island and protect it.

The young architect was Nicholas Joseph Clayton, born in Ireland and summoned to Galveston by Mr. Marx and Harris Kempner, Galveston business partners who wanted Clayton to design and supervise the construction of a hotel to replace the old Tremont Hotel, which had burned in 1865. "With its rotunda and Corinthian columns, Italian marble floors, and grand staircase, the second Tremont became the finest hotel in the South," writes Gary Cartwright.

Charmed by the Island, Clayton decided to stay and make his home in Galveston. By designing many of the great structures on the Strand, including the W. L. Moody building, the Marx and Kempner building, and the Hutchings-Sealy Bank, as well as spectacular homes and churches, he, in a forty-year period, significantly changed the face and the form of the city.

"Many Island homes stood on stilts and looked as fragile as grasshoppers ready to scatter. But this was the age of Nicholas Clayton too, and the churches, cathedrals and synagogues were oversized and wonderfully ostentatious," continues Cartwright. This was not surprising, as the rising young architect was a compulsive doodler, most often of church windows, altars, and steeples. Even mundane buildings, such as warehouses, revealed a trace of Victorian Gothic, so it was hard to tell if they were crypts or just plain storage places.

Clayton's career benefited from an "ongoing battle among the new elite to see who could build the Isle's grandest mansion, and the winner was Colonel Walter Gresham . . . The mammoth structure that Clayton designed for Gresham and his wife at the corner of 14th Street and Broadway was a gray sandstone and granite fortress with four-story turrets, topped with the winged horses of Assyria, a trio of tiled cones . . ." Garlanded with balconies and bristling with chimneys, it is now known as the Bishop's Palace. This fantasy in stone would cost more than $16 million to build today.

Most of Galveston's fashionable lived on Broadway. It was "the place to see and be seen, a street of elegant homes set along a wide esplanade planted with oaks, oleanders, and palms imported from the West Indies. Streetcar tracks ran along the esplanade, between these borders of tropical foliage, and at night people sat on their galleries or gathered on street corners and watched the so-called 'pretty cars' pass, strung with multi-colored electric lights and filled with young people singing and laughing," explains Cartwright.

Nicholas Clayton was the father of five children—all B.O.I.s. David McComb shares an anecdote that sums up Clayton's contribution to the Island. When the architect died at age seventy-seven in 1916, deeply in debt, his widow confided to Rabbi Henry Cohen that the family could not afford a proper headstone for his grave. Said the rabbi, himself a keystone figure in Isle history, "Oh, you don't need one, my dear Mary Lorena. He's got them all over town. Just go around and read some cornerstones."

Dreamer, designer, doodler, definer of the character of a city—Nicholas Clayton's works will forever reflect those heady Victorian glory days on the Isle, when the West was young, cotton was king, and Galveston was the proud "Wall Street of the Southwest."

*St. Mary's Cathedral's twin towers stand guard in front of the Nicholas
Clayton-designed center tower, crowned by St. Mary, Star of the Sea.*
—Robert John Mihovil

*Henry Rosenberg was born in Switzerland and came to Galveston at
age nineteen in 1843. When he died in 1893, a portion of his will read,
"I give 30,000 for the creation of not less than ten drinking fountains
for man and beast in various portions of the city of Galveston, locations
to be selected by my executors."*

—Courtesy the Rosenberg Library

Henry Rosenberg Quenched More Than the Thirst for Knowledge

Most Galvestonians know the name of Henry Rosenberg, a native of Switzerland who moved to Galveston at the age of nineteen in 1843, scarcely four years after Galveston was incorporated as a city, and made a fortune in railroading.

Naturally, his name is most closely associated with Rosenberg Library, that imposing neo-Classical building at 23rd and Sealy streets, established at the turn of the century through Rosenberg's will. And anyone who has ever waited out the interminable red light at 25th and Broadway has seen his name on the Texas Heroes' Monument, which he also funded. He was the major contributor to the Eaton Chapel at Trinity Episcopal Church and donated its handsome stained-glass window, "The Good Shepherd." He also gave funds to build the Rosenberg School, the Galveston Orphans Home, Grace Episcopal Church, The Galveston YMCA—and last but certainly not least, especially during the torpid Isle summers—The Rosenberg Drinking Fountains.

Originally, there were seventeen of the ornate granite fountains, designed to slake both human and equine thirsts. Water spouted from the top of each fountain, where people could get at it, then flowed into a trough at its base, where horses could lap it up.

The first Rosenberg fountains were erected in March 1898. Each of the city's twelve wards got one. Later, in October of the same year, five larger and more costly fountains were erected in Sherman Park, Central Park, and Morris Lasker Park; one near the Union Railway Station; and another on 20th Street. That last fountain, at the Beach Hotel, actually provided ice water. It had a vault with two-inch, cast-iron pipes running across it, where ice was placed daily to provide a cool drink of water.

The fountains were designed by J. Massy Rhind, of New York, and made of light-gray granite ornamented with bronze. Each fountain bore the inscription: "Gift of Henry Rosenberg." Eventually, the fountains outlived their usefulness, as automobiles replaced horses on the city streets and the heavy granite drinking troughs took up valuable space in a growing city. Most of the fountains were dismantled, with pieces of the distinctive gray granite gracing gardens and backyards across the Island. Eventually, only one of Rosenberg's fountains remained in its original spot, on Seawall Boulevard at 31st Street.

However, in the 1990s the scattered remains of the fountains were being collected at the Railroad Museum, and by 1996 enough pieces had been gathered to reconstruct one of the fountains, at 21st and Postoffice streets, across from the 1894 Grand Opera House.

Henry Rosenberg made his fortune in young, boisterous Galveston, and he took great pains to thank his adopted home through generous gifts of education and culture. But with his seventeen gray granite drinking fountains, the philanthropist from the cool Alps acknowledged the need of this sun-splashed sandbar's residents to quench more than their spiritual thirsts.

LeRoy Columbo Never Heard a Cry for Help—But He Answered Nearly a Thousand

AN ESSAY BY PEP VALDES

He lived in a bright and silent world, a world in motion and alive with the pulse of the ocean and the cheers of a soundless crowd. He swam like a dolphin, scurried on the sand like a crab, and saved the lives of nearly one thousand swimmers in trouble.

His smile warmed the beachfront, and his feats earned him a place in history. He was LeRoy Columbo, deaf-mute, champion swimmer, and super-lifeguard.

LeRoy was born in 1905 in a Galveston still devastated by the 1900 hurricane. As he grew up, the Island grade-raising was underway, and the new seawall was inching its way to the west.

At age seven LeRoy contracted spinal meningitis. Ravaging his young body, the disease took his hearing and left his legs useless.

His young brothers, Nick and Jacinto, put LeRoy's hands behind their necks, and the trio wore a path in the alley behind their home trying to stimulate and strengthen the helpless legs.

As the limbs improved, Nick and Jacinto hauled LeRoy to the Gulf, where the buoyant seawater cradled the boy as life returned to his legs. Soon he was more comfortable in the water than on land.

As a teen-ager, LeRoy tried out for the exclusive Surf Toboggan Club. Dues were 25 cents a week, and members were known for being the best swimmers of the city. LeRoy easily passed the initiation of swimming for three hours without stopping or floating and was soon to become the club's greatest champion.

His feats seemed superhuman; he once swam thirty miles, from San Luis Pass to the piers on the East End, in sixteen hours and twenty-four minutes! Hours ahead of his competition, he would spring from the water, fresh and seemingly ready to swim

LeRoy Columbo reputedly saved almost 1,000 lives, but his own life ended while he was living in a derelict car, penniless and embittered. His honors and awards came after his death in 1973 at age sixty-eight.
—Courtesy the Rosenberg Library

again. He won every distance race between 1929 and 1939 and was competing even into his fifties.

Once, a race was canceled because of rough weather—so he jumped in and swam the entire length of the course just to prove it could be done. It is said that during Prohibition LeRoy swam cases of bootleg liquor in to the beach from boats offshore.

Murdoch's Bathhouse and Bill Curry's Coaster Station rented floats to the public and served as the gathering place for LeRoy and his tanned friends. From Curry's, they would scan the water for swimmers in trouble.

Columbo rescued his first victim when he was twelve years old. Those who knew him said he had a sixth sense, that he did not need to hear cries for help to know when a swimmer was in trouble. He knew the ocean, understood the water and currents. He sensed the danger, knew the signs of someone in distress. By the time others realized a swimmer was drowning, LeRoy was often halfway there.

One summer day in 1942, on a beach crowded with soldiers, LeRoy was credited with saving nineteen lives.

His most dramatic rescue took place on Pier 20 when a tugboat, the *Propeller,* exploded into fire near where Columbo stood. When a nearby firehose crumbled, he dove into the water and pulled two crewmen from the flames. One was the tug's chief engineer, Fred W. Barr.

Fellow Surf Toboggan member Ducky Prendergast said, "LeRoy's life was on the beach"—and it was, for all of his sixty-eight years.

His last post was from 53rd to 61st streets, where the Noon Optimists erected a statue at 54th and Seawall in 1974 commemorating his record of the most lives saved by one person—907—a record that still stands.

LeRoy Columbo: A true local legend who spent his days in the service of others drawn to the sand, the water, and the sun that all come together so invitingly on this little isle we call Galveston.

—G.F.B.

Charlie Bertolino: Father, Fisherman, Friend to All

There is a monument on Broadway at 14th Street dedicated to an extraordinary man. He was a pied piper, a baker, a fisherman, a lifesaver; he fed the poor and hungry. He was a devoted son and husband, and to this day he is loved and respected by his descendants.

Of course, we are talking about Charles Bertolino, Sr. Born in 1887 on Galveston Island, he was one of six sons of parents who came here from Italy.

He made an unforgettable mark on this island.

In his early boyhood, Charlie became the "pied piper of Galveston" when rats became a severe problem on the Island. Always on the lookout for ways to earn money, he heard that a bounty of 5 cents per rat was being offered. So, fashioning his own traps—the proverbial "better mousetrap," no doubt—he went to work. But as fortune, or misfortune, would have it, he caught so many rats that the city fathers didn't have enough money to pay him.

Fishing was his trade, but he also was a baker at Grenard's Bakery at 13th and Avenue L. His talents as a fisherman were legend. As a baker—well, some of the loaves were not exactly the right shape. But they were good and fresh and hot, and he was allowed to take the rejects home. That, with his fishing expertise, enabled him to share his catch of seafood and a loaf of bread with many other families.

Quite naturally, Charlie fell in love with a Galveston girl. He married his Mable when she entered her fifteenth year. They made 10th Street their home—after all, Charlie had been raised on 10th and M. When the children started arriving, one or two each year, Charlie's mother came to live with them to help with the kids. As the little family grew to become a large family, older siblings would help with the little ones. Final count: Twenty-one children, including four sets of twins.

Charlie settled into a routine. He started each morning with a cup of coffee and a piece of buttered bread, then headed off to the

Pied piper, baker, fisherman, lifesaver . . . Charlie Bertolino made an unforgettable mark on this island.
—Courtesy Ruby Bertolino Roberts

South Jetty for his five-mile swim to Murdoch's Pier. Then it was back to East Beach, and with his 1,000-foot seine net, he went to work. And work it was: He had to set and retrieve that net three or four times a day to make a living for his ever-growing family.

The stories abound. During the 1915 Storm, as a strong twenty-eight-year-old, he rowed a skiff through the raging, flooded streets of Galveston, pulling survivors aboard until exhaustion overcame him. You could always recognize Charlie. A true fisherman, he never wore a belt but used a rope to hold up his pants. A mop of curly black hair was twisted with a piece of hemp twine to keep it out of his eyes.

Charlie became a tourist attraction as he seined the waters of the Gulf. And a bit of a showoff he was: As the vacationers watched in awe, he would skin catfish with his teeth and eat raw shrimp. When someone wanted to buy a dozen live blue crabs, he would plunge bare hands into the barrel of grasping, pinching sharp claws and count them out, one by one.

There wasn't a sports fishing channel on TV to let fishermen know the fishing conditions—all Charlie had to do was walk up 10th Street to the Gulf and he would know exactly what fish would be running that day. He'd holler to his sons (and there were fourteen of them) to "load up"—and the hunt was on. At one time, when the weather was freezing and the fishing was very bad, his mother held a prayer vigil. Charlie came home with the catch of his life—so many fish that the neighbors for blocks around were invited to share in this "miracle" catch. Other days, when food was not so plentiful, a single knife blade of peanut butter could make up to a dozen sandwiches—all Mable did was spread and scrape, spread and scrape. Everyone could have a taste of peanut butter.

As a weatherman, Charlie was relied on. No one in the neighborhood would even think of boarding up their windows for a storm—that is, until they saw Charlie and the boys working on their house. Then they knew a storm was on its way.

Family reunions were held every Sunday at Bertolino's. The highlight of the week—huge pots of steaming spaghetti and black skillets simmering with spicy spaghetti sauce, ready to smother hundreds of succulent meatballs. With seven daughters and assorted daughters-in-law, there were many cooks, and never was the broth spoiled. Homemade wine was ladled out of a giant, cheesecloth-covered crock; the little old winemaker—none other than Charlie's mother, Grandma Rosalee.

Working the Gulf surf day after day as he did, Charlie was often the first one to spot swimmers in trouble, and his lifesaving feats would fill a whole book. He pulled more than five hundred distressed souls from the hungry Gulf waters. State Senator "Babe" Schwartz drafted a resolution, passed by the Texas Senate, commending Charlie's service. No one has counted the medals awarded him by the American Red Cross, and he was presented two citations for bravery by President Franklin Delano Roosevelt.

Charlie and Mable Bertolino left more than one hundred children, grandchildren, great-grandchildren, and even great-great-grandchildren. It is in families like this, always looking out for others even as they shoulder their own particular burdens, that we see the courage, determination, and love that define the breed of humanity we call "Galvestonian."

You Don't Cuss at Sonny's Place ...
and You Don't Shoot at Junior!

What does Galveston have in common today with New York City or San Francisco? Well, we are all situated on the water—but there used to be something else: We all had lots of "Mom and Pop" neighborhood groceries and taverns. Those big cities still boast hundreds of little corner cafés, grocery stores, and bars that have managed to hold out against the fast food places, singles clubs, and grocery chains that have driven the little family businesses out elsewhere.

In Galveston as well, there used to be little neighborhood places like Al's Cafe, John's Grocery, the Family Inn—but big business has just about squeezed Mom and Pop to death here. That is not to say there aren't some stubborn survivors—Junior Puccetti, for instance.

Jim Brigance related in the *Galveston Daily News:*

Junior's parents turned the ground floor of their home at 19th Street and Avenue L into a neighborhood tavern in 1937. Junior leased it out but in 1944 decided to run the place himself. It was, and still is, a quiet neighborhood bar and cafe called Sonny's Place . . . ice-cold beer, best hamburgers and shrimp burgers in town, sports on the TV—and cussing will get you thrown out.

In the fall of 1971, three hijackers probably had the idea that a little Mom and Pop place would be an easy score. But it nearly cost these amateurs their lives.

It was a Friday night. Three men were sitting at the bar, and nineteen other customers were at tables and booths, most listening to the high school football game on the radio. At about 9:30, three men walked in . . . one stood at the door . . . two confronted Junior at the bar. Brandishing a .45, one robber ordered, "Give me all the money!"

"Take it easy," Junior responded as he began emptying the cash register. All the customers were on the floor as gunman number two demanded their wallets and purses. Junior said the first guy swung his pistol around and it hit a napkin container on the bar, accidentally discharging and throwing a slug into the counter. Pretending to be hit and falling to the floor, Junior's son quickly

Junior Puccetti still serves from his bullet-scarred bar, and the menu still reminds customers of the "no cussin'" rule.

—Courtesy Junior Puccetti

pitched him a .38 revolver from the kitchen. Customer Edward Connelly, worried that Junior had been hit, stood up and was whacked over the head with a shotgun barrel. Then the gunfight ensued. One slug hit the beer spigot—there's still a dent in it.

The robbers grabbed $125 and fled with Junior in hot pursuit, emptying his gun at them as they ran down the street. Junior said he'd always worried about being robbed, although he never had been before—or since. He said he would have given them the money, but when the gun went off, well . . . !

The big gun battle of 1971 is commemorated to this day with an inscribed plaque on the bar, next to the bullet hole in the countertop. But it should serve as more than just a brass plaque recollection of a beer-joint shootout. It ought to be a billboard saying that the Mom and Pop places may all get steam-rollered out of business one of these days, but it won't be by nickel-and-dime punks. At least not as long as there are people like Junior Puccetti.

So next time you see a little bread-and-milk grocery, or a family tavern on the corner where neighbors gather, give Mom and

Pop a hand for holding out. And make sure there's a buck or two in it. Buy something. They're still tough today, just like they used to be—because that's the legacy of the people who took root on a sea-swept sandbar and built a city we call Galveston.

To Savvas and Katina, Whose Grasp Exceeded Their Dreams

Galveston has been greatly influenced by immigrants who came here to live from all over the world. There were Russians, Swiss, Scots, Czechs, Germans, Greeks, and Norwegians. They came from Boston, the Carolinas, New York, England, France, Germany, Ireland, and Italy.

One of these was a young man who was born in Greece, in a small mountain village near Tripoli. The youngest of four children, he lived with his family on one acre of land, where they raised goats. None of them went to school. Although the tiny village was beautiful, the poverty was harsh. When his father died, Savvas saw no chance there for a better life, one that involved more than tending to the goats.

Savvas had heard stories from his uncles about the United States and how wonderful it was. As he was the bold one, the rebel in the family, he made plans to immigrate to the United States. His dream was not the promise of riches for himself, but the promise of an education for the family he knew he would have someday. He wanted his children to have a better life and more educational opportunities. When Savvas was twenty-one, he left his mother, two brothers, and a sister, never to see them again, and boarded a ship that brought him to Ellis Island in New York Harbor.

As the railroads were extending their tracks rapidly across the United States, strong young immigrants were hired for the work gangs. Savvas' first stop was in Arkansas, and then on to Utah. The Greek gang foreman took a liking to

A newly married Savvas and Katina engaged in a board game. Their dreams of the future would more than come true.

—Courtesy George P. Mitchell

Savvas and taught him some reading and some writing—not much, but enough so that he could stay in touch with his family in Greece.

Savvas had a cousin in Texas who ran a shoeshine parlor in Houston. Business was very good, so Savvas joined him, and the two opened a second parlor. There were many Greek immigrants in the South, and one day Savvas was looking at a Greek-language newspaper (he still did not read very well) and saw a picture of a beautiful young lady. She had come to Florida from Greece to visit her sister. Savvas tore the picture out of the paper, put it in his pocket, and decided he must meet this beauty. Savvas had a great sense of style—I guess you would say he was a dapper young man—so he put on his best bib and tucker and headed for Tarpon Springs, Florida.

He found the beautiful girl, but what a disappointment: Her sister had already picked a fiancé for her. But Savvas was not dismayed. His charm and boldness captivated Katina, and before he returned to Texas he had convinced her to come to Houston to marry him. Soon after their marriage, the young couple decided to come to Galveston and open up yet another shoeshine parlor.

Life in Galveston was good. In 1911 their first child, a son, was born, followed by two more boys and finally a girl. Savvas and Katina worked hard to raise their growing family. And Savvas never lost sight of the reason he left Greece—the dream that his children would have an education. Although Katina never learned English and Savvas spoke only a little, the children were taught to concentrate on good grades, knowing they all would have to work to put themselves through school.

And the opportunity for education that Savvas never had was indeed available to his children. Each went on to earn college degrees—one in journalism, one in chemical engineering, one a double degree in geology and petroleum engineering, and little Maria earned her degree in liberal arts. Their alma maters were Baylor, the University of Texas, and Texas A&M. True Texans all.

Savvas and Katina didn't plan it or know it, but they left a legacy—you might even say a dynasty: A family, children and now grandchildren, dedicated to education, hard work, and success.

Katina and Savvas—known to us on the Island as Katina and Mike Mitchell, parents of Isle journalist and restaurateur Christie Mitchell, Johnny Mitchell, Maria Mitchell, and oil and gas magnate George Mitchell—your dreams really did come true, and Galveston Island is all the richer for it.

Two Mayors, One Island, and a Wealth of History

Once upon a time, this island had two mayors, and both were right here in Galveston.

Of course, everyone here knew Mayor Herbert Y. Cartwright— a politician's politician who defeated incumbent Mayor George W. Fraser in the 1947 election, at the tender age of thirty-two. He ran as a candidate against gambling and prostitution, which were then rampant on the Isle, and served as a mayor in support of this "underground economy." Chubby and friendly, Cartwright eventually personally handed out nine thousand business cards bearing his trademark slogan, "Thanks a million!"

But not everyone knew the Mayor of Fairville. Still, the two mayors became friends and corresponded regularly. The Mayor of Fairville was a versatile fellow—not only did he hold the title of mayor, but he also published a weekly newspaper. Maybe it wasn't as big as the *Galveston Daily News,* but it was every bit as exciting and interesting to its subscribers. When Mayor Cartwright found out his friend, the Mayor of Fairville, was publishing a newspaper and needed a typewriter, he sent him one. The Mayor of Fairville even delivered his paper to all subscribers and collected the money as well.

The newspaper carried neighborhood items of great interest, and also stories of Galveston history. You see, the Mayor of Fairville had inherited a love of history from a grandfather, who shared his great interest in history with his family, and in turn from his father, who would often take his young son on an outing for the day.

Their favorite places to visit would be cemeteries, where they would search for the graves of early settlers—and the tombstones would provide the basis for history lessons from father to son. These history lessons became stories to tell, and the Mayor of Fairville painstakingly pecked them out on the typewriter in the seclusion of his office—a small, wood-frame building covered with palm fronds that blended into the lush tropical plantings of Fairville.

Now, the thirty-two-year-old mayor of Galveston may have seemed young for the job, but the Mayor of Fairville was probably the youngest mayor of any town in this area—real or imagined. Because, yes, Fairville was an imaginary town, and the Mayor of Fairville a very real ten-year-old boy. A boy so many of us knew as Maury Darst.

Herbert Cartwright, a tennis hustler who came of age among the bootleggers and whorehouses of wide-open Galveston, served five years as mayor in the late forties and early fifties, then won another term in 1955 when the city changed from the commission form of government to its current mayor-council system.

Maury Darst, of the palm-covered "office," and mayor of his own youthful imagining, grew up to become a well-known historian. After graduating in the first class to attend the new Ball High School on Avenue O, he went on to college, where he earned a master's degree, with history as his major and journalism as his minor. He taught history at Galveston College, lectured at Texas A&M University, and—not at all surprisingly—worked at the *Galveston Daily News*.

When Maury Darst died so suddenly in 1990, only fifty-three years old, he left behind a wealth of history—a gaping hole in the Island's institutional memory—and a remembrance of a time when the Oleander City had two mayors, a most unlikely pairing even for our beautiful, romantic, historic (and at times a bit off-the-wall) Galveston Island.

Maury Darst, young mayor of Fairville, is delighted with the typewriter sent to him by Galveston Mayor Herbert Cartwright. Meanwhile, Herbie relaxes on a plane trip to conduct business in Washington, D.C.
—Courtesy Elizabeth Darst

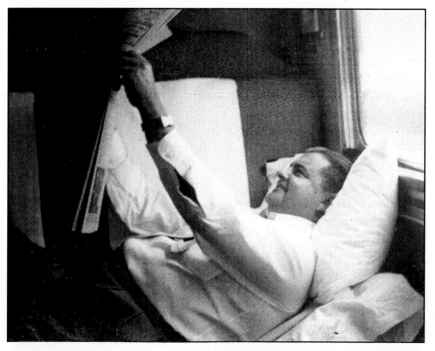

Some are Islanders, Some Just Live Here ...

AN ESSAY BY MAX RIZLEY, JR.

MOVING AGAIN—"Why don't you move off this island?" my mother moaned as she dodged the small Niagara in the stairwell next to my apartment and picked her way through the soggy plaster fragments of ceiling scattered about the second-floor landing.

"Just up to Clear Lake, someplace a little more protected," my father added. "Look at this place. It's a mess. Why would you subject yourself to this?"

I had a brief sense of déjà vu. We had had this same conversation in 1983, when Hurricane Alicia trashed the Seawall apartment I was living in then. This time, it was 1989, and an otherwise forgettable storm named Jerry had brought the roof down.

Why, indeed? I strained my mind for a moment in search of an answer for my parents, and, finding none that they—nor any off-Islanders—would understand, just gave them the same withering glare I did back in '83.

Move off the Island? Out of the question, of course. Case closed.

But why? What mysterious force, what kind of electromagnetic field, does this little sandbar emit that holds its residents to it even when common sense would say "give it up"? It's something I've been pondering ever since that long-ago conversation.

There are some easy answers—how often have you heard, "Ah'm a fawth-generation Islandah; Ah'm a Bee-Oh-Eye, bawn at St. Mary's Infirmary, an' Ah nevah bin across the Causeway!"

A tree rooted that deeply isn't going to give in to some storm or the occasional economic slump.

But for every "fawth-generation Islandah," there had to once be a first-generation Islander who could have headed for the plains after the first hurricane, but didn't. What was it that kept him—that keeps us latter-day "first-generation Islanders"—here, even as the roof falls in around us?

It's not the lack of Houston traffic, it's not the quaint ginger-

Two miles out in the Gulf of Mexico, floating like a giant lily pad, is a sunny sandbar called Galveston Island.

—Robert John Mihovil

bread houses, it's not the beaches and the pastel-tinged Gulf sunrises; would that it were that simple, because then I would have an answer my father and mother could understand. Oh, that all enters into it, of course, but the real answer is in the heart rather than the geography.

There is a deep-seated difference between someone who lives on Galveston Island and an Islander. Lots of people buy houses here, or rent apartments here, and they may truly like the place; still, they'll move out tomorrow if a better job opens up, up the freeway somewhere. They hear the gentle crash of the surf, and it's a nice sound, but, hey, they can take it or leave it if times get tough.

The Islander hears that same surf, but he hears voices in it, voices of his kindred spirits—the voices of people who felt instinctively, as soon as they set foot on the Island, that here was the one place that someone with pluck, with an independent spirit, could be at home.

They sensed the very soul of the Island, the quiet tenacity of a place that, exposed, wave-battered, and windblown, stood its ground and challenged Nature to uproot it; they sensed that soul, and it spoke to their hearts. It challenged them, it threw down a gauntlet, and they picked it up.

Those first Islanders did more than just move here, they cast their lots with the Island. They entwined their fates with Galveston's—come hurricane, come fire, come yellow fever.

And whether or not he is of their blood, today's Islander is of Them. He feels Them watching him, watching him and wondering, as he surveys the soggy mess left by the last storm, whether he will pick up the pieces and dig in a little deeper, or whether he will turn his back and flee to drier precincts. Is he an Islander, or is he just passing through?

"You know," my father was saying, "There're some nice apartments up in Clear Lake. And there's all kinds of jobs opening up there around NASA. There's nothing here for you." He cast a baleful glance at a dangling tuft of pink ceiling insulation.

Nothing here? My God, can't you see Them? Can't you hear Them? Me, leave Galveston? And let Them down?

PART III

Blood, Sweat, and Tears

Ashton Villa: Grande Dame of Galveston's "Broadway Beauties"

Who hasn't admired Galveston's "Broadway Beauties"?

They are three, these "Broadway Beauties"—the 1859 Ashton Villa, the 1886 Bishop's Palace, and the 1895 Willis-Moody Mansion, stately homes that reflect the opulent lifestyles enjoyed by Galveston's wealthiest families from before the Civil War, through the Victorian era, and into the early twentieth century.

Today's Galveston Beach Band concerts take place in Mary Moody Northen Plaza, with the red-brick back of Ashton Villa as a backdrop.

The winds of change were blowing hard in 1859, says long-time Isle writer Steve Long. That was the year Oregon became America's thirty-third state. Abolitionist John Brown staged his ill-fated raid on the federal arsenal at Harper's Ferry, West Virginia. Daniel Emmett wrote a stirring song called "Dixie," and Charles Gounod's opera *Faust* was first performed. The first successful oil well in the United States was drilled in Pennsylvania. At the age of thirty-eight, Col. James Moreau Brown built a home in Galveston. For nearly a century and a half, his Ashton Villa has been a symbol of the Island's architectural elegance and grace.

Unlike the other two Broadway Beauties, both built in the late nineteenth century, Ashton Villa predates the Civil War. The

Born in 1859, almost a century and a half old, Ashton Villa remains an elegant Broadway Beauty.

—Courtesy Galveston Historical Foundation

two-story, nine-room house was built largely by slave labor. It took Colonel Brown, who was president of the Galveston, Houston and Henderson Railroad, and his workers a year to build the home in what was then a growing city of 8,000 people.

Walking through the doors evokes visions of women in hoop skirts and men dressed in the gray of the Confederacy. The Gold Room, the largest room in Ashton Villa, sparkles with gilt furnishings and speaks of the lavish cotillions, elegant coming-out parties, and lively Mardi Gras balls that were the benchmarks of genteel Island life in the nineteenth century.

Ashton Villa was most noted for its gala entertainment when the Brown children grew up. One of them, Miss Bettie Brown, was a world traveler and an accomplished painter. She smoked—scandalous for those days—and she never married.

Eventually, Ashton Villa fell out of the hands of the Brown family and by the 1960s was home to Galveston's El Mina Shriners. The Shriners' move to other quarters, and the subsequent threat that Ashton Villa would now suffer the same fate as so many of her long-vanished neighbors, was a catalyst for Galveston's historic preservation movement of the 1960s and 1970s. Spared from the wrecking ball and lovingly restored, Ashton Villa is today the grande dame of the Isle's "Broadway Beauties."

And oh, yes—it is said that Miss Bettie's vivacious spirit still visits Ashton Villa to look at her paintings, photographs, and mementoes. Who knows? Maybe she will quietly join you when you step back into the past and visit this lovely Broadway Beauty.

Isle's "Old Lady" Made as Much History as She Reported

Ernest Hemingway may have had his "Old Man and The Sea," but Galveston Island has its own "Old Lady by the Sea." Born on April 11, 1842, the affectionately named "Old Lady" is *The Galveston Daily News*. During the early days of the Texas Republic, as many as eighteen papers started in Galveston. Only the *Daily News* has survived.

In 1842 a single copy of the *News* cost 6½ cents. In 1963 the daily price went down to a nickel a copy. By 1969 the price had doubled to a dime; in 1977 the cost was two bits; and by 1997 it was 50 cents a copy. Naturally, the newspaper that has told the

The Galveston Daily News, *founded in 1842, was the first newspaper to occupy a building created exclusively for use as a newspaper publishing plant. This building, designed by Nicholas Clayton, in the 2100 block of Mechanic, was home to the* News *until it moved west in 1965.*
—Courtesy the Rosenberg Library

stories of Galveston since the days of the Republic has a few stories of its own.

One of the first editors, an ex-schoolteacher who held that post from 1844 to 1875, was an astute and frugal manager. So frugal, indeed, the story goes, that he had two copies of the paper delivered to his home each day, and after he and his wife had read them, he refolded both papers, carried them to the office, and had them resold.

During the nineteenth century, the *News* was run on "nag-power." Beginning in 1885, the paper used a horse or mule on a treadmill to operate its new mechanized printing press. Steam technology already existed but required a vast and reliable amount of fresh water—and the *News* could not depend on its cistern to supply the voracious thirst of a boiler. The treadmill ran through a hole cut in the back of the newspaper's building; the press only stopped long enough to give Charlie, the horse, a chance to get a drink.

In fact, the presses rarely stopped, no matter what the power source—quite a feat in a city that had been ravaged by war, fire, and especially hurricanes. The *News* was out with a one-page edition the day after the great 1900 hurricane that killed 6,000 people on the Island. The simple sheet carried mainly names of confirmed casualties. And when the mighty 1915 Storm knocked out electricity in Galveston, the *News'* presses rolled on—powered by a chain connected to the drive shaft of the newspaper's delivery truck.

Back in the early 1800s, news was carried by letter, and most letters arrived via sailing ship from New Orleans—a far cry from today, when national and international headlines arrive in the blink of a byte via the big satellite dish that sits beside the *News'* front door. The paper was an early player in satellite-transmitted news—but then, it boasts of many firsts. The first labor union local in Texas was the printers' "chapel" at the *News*. The paper installed the first telephone in Texas in 1878, linking the newsroom with the editor's home. In 1881 the *News* built a little railroad engine and car to carry its papers from Galveston to Houston. The run was fifty straight, flat miles, and speeds often reached seventy to eighty miles per hour. The early-morning run, which included a slow crossing over a trestle spanning the bay and several stops, took about fifty minutes. Two years later, a special train operated to carry the *News* throughout Texas. This was the first daily train of its kind in the world.

In 1959 Lillian Herz, a longtime writer and columnist for the *News*, wrote that "so important a place did the *News* occupy in the annals of journalism that its style and composition were copied by the publisher of the *New York Times,* recognized as the world's greatest newspaper."

Quite a tribute for a little hometown daily, deeply rooted in the sand—and history—of Galveston Island, Texas.

Isle's Heart Beats in Historic Neighborhoods

So. You say you've visited the *Elissa* and toured the Bishop's Palace. You've seen a play at the Grand Opera House. And, of course, you've walked the Strand, maybe sat down in front of the Emporium and watched the passing parade of humanity. Now you're ready to head home and tell everyone how you explored all the historic treasures of Galveston Island.

Well, guess again—unless you found time to cover the 300 square blocks that comprise the Island's historical residential neighborhoods—some 1,500 Victorian homes in all.

Many newcomers to Galveston assume that, aside from a few monolithic mansions and business houses, there is little left on the Isle predating 1900, when the Great Storm of that year presumably wiped this vulnerable little sandbar clean.

But there is plenty of Victorian whimsy to be found in Galveston, on the side streets beyond and behind the famed "Broadway Beauties." And for the price of a little shoe leather, you can truly say you've seen the beating heart of historic Galveston—the fanciful nineteenth-century neighborhoods where twenty-first-century Galveston hangs its hat.

To truly appreciate the clever beauty of Victorian Galveston, you must take the time to walk leisurely through the tree-lined streets, for only on foot can you see what surprises lie behind the lush greenery of oleander bushes, honeysuckle vines, and palmetto trees. There probably is not another place in the country where you can walk for miles and view so many authentic nineteenth-century homes, side by side, sometimes lined up ten to the block.

George Osborne stops his horse and carriage at the corner of 17th and Ball, creating a frozen moment in time.

—Robert John Mihovil

Stop as you stroll and study the details of the houses, from the "widow's walks" on the rooftops, the decorated fascias, bargeboards, gallery railings, and long stairways, to the ornate wrought-iron fences that encase and enhance the narrow lots. Note the individual touches on the homes—a towering pillar here, shadowed silhouettes of ornate carvings there, a splash of stained glass in a window, or a wide, welcoming porch, reminders of Galveston's "Gilded Age" of hospitality and charm.

The Victorian homes range from small, simple cottages to large, elaborate mansions. Many have been lovingly restored to their original Gilded Age exuberance by romantic people wanting something with more soul than suburbia's cookie-cutter tract houses; others, while sorely wanting the touch of a paintbrush, proclaim their vitality with toddlers' toys strewn about a gap-toothed porch and carefully tended tomato vines flanking a sagging stairway.

The architecture reflects a variety of styles and periods, the earliest being examples of the Greek Revival style, built during the 1850s. I make no pretense of being a student of architecture, but I can't help being fascinated with the angles of the eaves, turrets, cupolas, shutters, and the play of light and shadow on the lacy woodwork. Let your mind erase the modern touches, such as TV antennas, air conditioners, or metal hurricane blinds, and step back in time to really see the original dignity and beauty of these old homes.

These Victorian homes have lived through periods of immense prosperity and survived the Island's occupation by hostile armies, fires, economic malaise, neglect, and storms of devastating power. Their presence is a testimony not only to the strength of their structures, but also to the vision and determination of this tiny island's citizenry.

Moreover, they illustrate clearly why Galveston is known as a city with a glorious history and special charm—a city just waiting to share those charms. So turn a corner, park the car, and take a walk through Victorian Galveston to truly discover the glory that was, and is, such a wonderful part of Galveston Island.

The 1900 Storm: A Shattered City, A Strengthened People

If there's one fact about Galveston that even the most off–off-Islander can call to mind, it is that a terrible hurricane in 1900 killed thousands and ranks as the worst natural disaster in American history. Volumes have been written over the years about that horrific September day; to rehash here the tales of who survived by clinging to which treetop, or how many miles inland the storm's fury drove oceangoing ships, is not our object here.

But as the storm's fury abated, as the all-engulfing sea drained back to "its own appointed limits," it left behind more than splintered wreckage and stinking mud. People, too, emerged from the

With their few remaining possessions, survivors of the storm sloshed through flooded streets determined to rebuild their beloved city.
—Courtesy the Galveston County Museum

storm's soggy leavings; people and, incredibly, a city—battered and broken, to be sure, but still very much alive.

Galveston in the late 1800s had a cavalier attitude about hurricanes, regarding them more as inconveniences, rather than as the truly deadly threat they really were. Most adults had, after all, ridden out three big blows. One in 1871 washed a schooner and three sloops up 19th Street and partially wrecked St. Patrick's Church. In 1875 a storm drove thirteen-foot tides across the entire Island, and eleven years later the 1886 Storm—which erased the bustling port city of Indianola from the Texas map—tore off a few roofs in Galveston, flattened some fences, and, as usual, washed away the Strand's wooden paving blocks. There was some talk of building a seawall, but no one took it seriously. Islanders assumed Galveston had stood up against the worst Nature could throw at them.

However, they would discover that Nature always has worse to offer.

History has recorded the fury and destruction of the catastrophic storm of 1900. With a storm tide of more than fifteen feet above normal, and twenty-five-foot breakers on top of that crashing over the low, unprotected beaches, the hurricane smashed the frail wooden buildings along the first few blocks in from the beach, then used their debris as a battering ram to mow down anything in its path, virtually scraping the Isle clean on Saturday night, September 8.

Sunday morning, the 9th, saw a brilliant sunrise, the sky a clear blue, the Gulf calm and drowsy—a peaceful illusion, shattered as soon as one turned toward what had only yesterday been "The Queen City of the Gulf." As one exhausted survivor put it, "Strange, our only thought was how to win this disaster."

That morning, Mayor Walter Jones called an emergency meeting of city leaders at the Tremont Hotel. Isaac "Ike" Kempner, John Sealy, Morris Lasker, Rabbi Henry Cohen, and Father James Kirwin joined the Deep Water Committee, and the mayor designated them an ad hoc committee, empowered to do whatever they thought was necessary to put Galveston back on the map. The commitment to clean up and rebuild the city had been made.

By Wednesday, September 12, conditions in Galveston were reported as much improved. The water supply from the mainland was working, and while it could not be sent through all the mains, there was enough for all needs in those portions of the city where life and property had been left comparatively intact.

Thursday night's sleep made the beleaguered Galvestonians a new people. The difference in their appearance, in their energy, from only the day before, was noticed by all. Streets that had been empty and silent the previous day were filled with people. Women met on the corners in the residential areas with warm embraces as they found fellow survivors and spoke of their experiences on Saturday night. The men gathered and made plans for the future. By 10 A.M. the whole city was up and buoyant. The effect of that one night's sleep was marvelous. No longer was there talk of abandoning the city; the cry on the lips of all was that Galveston should be greater now than it had ever been. People who wouldn't have given ten dollars for the place on Wednesday were saying on Thursday that they would have given more for a Galveston lot then than before the storm.

Why? Because the pluck of the Island people came out after that night of rest. Galveston was stronger than ever by its weathering such a ferocious storm, the people said, and they began to speak of their own resolve. "We have withstood much, but the world will say we stood it well. If we can do as we have done through such a trial, what can we not do in the daily battle of life? Galveston shall be rebuilt!" one editorialist wrote.

And thousands of Islanders set to work cleaning up and rebuilding, asking nothing about wages—even those who had no property of their own left. Galvestonians were out to show the world the stuff they were made of. The storm could not kill the city, although it almost mortally wounded her. There was determination there. There was pride there. And above all, there were memories there for the people of Galveston, memories that would not be drowned in wave and wind.

While preparations for the great rebuilding lay ahead, work began immediately in the commercial heart of the Island City. Railroads and the waterfront were being rapidly cleared of ruins. The telephone and telegraph companies rushed to restore their services, and full telegraph service was re-established by the close of the week.

A well-known reporter from the *Dallas Morning News* arrived to inquire about the condition of the sister publication, the venerable *Galveston Daily News*. He found the *News'* office on Mechanic Street with its doors broken, the building flooded, engines and press damaged. Meeting with Major Robert Lowe, the *Daily News* general manager, he remarked that if he were Lowe, he would print the paper in Houston.

"You would, would you?" exploded Lowe. "Well, I won't!" He shook his fist and stamped the floor. "You never lived here. You don't know . . . and you would ask me to desert? No, no, no! This paper lives and dies with this town. We'll build it again—and the *News* will help." The newspaper did not miss an issue.

To be sure, there were people who moved away from Galveston, never to return. Most of the population, however, refused to give up. They were willing to stay on the Island through thick or thin—for all her faults and calamities, they still loved the little sandbar that some called Galveston, but they called home.

The Seawall: Robert's Rule for Nature

Viewed from the air above the Gulf of Mexico, rippling waves wash a smooth, wide, sandy beach—above which looms a solid gray wall, protecting an island city against that same sea's angrier moods.

The Galveston Island Seawall was conceived and built after the great hurricane of 1900 sent pulverizing waves crashing over the low sandbar that was Galveston, killing more than six thousand. The wall was built section by section as the city grew, until today it runs more than one hundred blocks, from land's end at Bolivar Roads, westward to Cove View Boulevard.

The cornerstone was laid in 1902, and by the time the last, westernmost section was finished in 1962, the wall was 10.4 miles long, covering one-third of the Isle's Gulf coastline. When it was all said and done, the Isle's beachfront was shielded by a wall of concrete seventeen feet wide at the base, rising sixteen feet above the mean high-tide line. At the top, the Seawall is capped with five feet of concrete; at its base, a twenty-seven-foot width of Texas red granite riprap staunches the force of most waves and tides before they ever reach the wall. The total cost: $14.5 million.

One of the three original army engineers brought in to oversee the Seawall project was General Henry M. Robert. As a young soldier, he had witnessed the tyranny of a presiding officer over a public discussion, and he developed a system of rules

Seawall Boulevard in 1904 boasted boardwalks and a railing and was a popular promenade for both citizens and visitors.

—Courtesy Galveston County Museum

to keep meetings of all kinds from descending into chaos. His now-famous book became the law for running democratic bodies throughout the world: *Robert's Rules of Order.*

As it turned out, he also knew something about ruling nature, and his "book" on that was written in granite and concrete along the Galveston beachfront.

During the Seawall's construction in the early part of the century, "it became popular to promenade atop the unfinished wall, especially on Sunday. Boys set up ladders and charged five cents to use them," writes David McComb. "A reporter commented that this form of enterprise would give Galveston a reputation for 'bleeding its excursionists.'"

Women and girls refused to stand on the wall, because that would require them to climb ladders. According to McComb, "In a day when ladies wore full skirts and the glimpse of an ankle was a thrill for men, ladders were a risque business. Yet, thousands of females wished to inspect 'their' wall and not all were forestalled." One young lady hurried up a ladder, then lifted herself a scant three more feet to the top, thinking no one was watching her. However, a gang of boys spied the ladder and sprinted to hold it for her to descend. But one thing a girl was afraid to do in those days was to climb down a ladder while a boy held it. Speeding down the wall for three hundred feet, she leaped off into a fairly soft mound of sand. Landing upright, she blew a kiss to the disappointed boys and vanished into a gray sea fog.

Today, throngs of people flock to the Seawall—it is one of our most popular attractions. They pedal two-, three-, and four-wheeled vehicles. They drive, bike, jog, and walk; some just sit and watch the sunrises and sunsets and listen to the swash of the sea as it laps at the sand and the pink granite riprap at the base of the Seawall. And many local Galvestonians are members of the "Seawall Brigade": They start their day with a walk along the Seawall, exchanging brief greetings with folks who only see each other between six and eight in the morning before going their separate ways.

Whether visitors or citizens of the Island, we feel as though we are standing at the edge of time when we stand on the Seawall and gaze in wonder upon the eternal vastness of the sea.

Islanders Won Their Home Back From the Sea in Grade-Raising

Galveston's Seawall: A solid gray barrier of tremendous proportions looming above the sandy beaches and standing guard against the sea, built after the devastating 1900 hurricane to protect the Island from nature's fiercest storms.

Building the Seawall was an engineering miracle—yet, even it was child's play compared to the task of raising the grade of the Island, bringing the city to a level that would place it and its people above the raging storm waves.

It was a task that, in terms of hardship and inconvenience, would shame even the very worst of today's highway-repair projects. Between 1902 and 1910, every house, every building, every church and school over an area of 500 blocks—more than 2,300 structures both grand and humble—all were raised on jackscrews and filled underneath with sand. Streets were torn apart and repaved. Streetcar tracks, water pipes, gas lines, trees, and even cemeteries had to be elevated. The grade would vary across the Island, from eight feet at the beach to three feet on West Broadway.

The enormity of the project posed a troubling question—where to find the eleven million cubic yards of sand necessary for the fill. A German engineer came up with a solution: Use sand from the ship channel, which needed dredging anyway. So five self-loading dredges were brought over from Germany, a canal was dug across the city, and work began. As houses were jacked up, dredges would move along the canal, discharging a liquid sand-and-water slurry through pipes. The sand settled, and the water ran back through the canal to the bay.

Despite many inconveniences, Islanders adjusted. Schoolboys made sport out of racing in front of the cannon-like pipes spewing mud and silt. In the heat of a summer afternoon, children crawled under the stilts of raised homes and played or read in the cool, damp shade. It became an acceptable practice for people to take shortcuts through the homes of strangers. Islanders learned to live with mud. Vehicles were allowed only where work

In 1905 Islanders were learning to live with muck as houses were raised and sand and mud were pumped beneath them. Rickety wooden walkways became the streets and sidewalks of the city.

—Courtesy Galveston County Museum

was finished, and traffic problems were always encountered at the drawbridges that spanned the canal. The drawbridges closed to street traffic at nine in the evening, and people who lingered too late at the beach were forced to use the ferry operated by the bridges' night tender, Admiral Billy Irwin.

More than 2,100 structures were raised, and more than sixteen million cubic yards of fill spread across the Island. It took 700 jackscrews to lift the newly restored, 3,000-ton St. Patrick's Church a mere five feet, but they did it, and not a single service was missed.

The grade-raising project took six of the strangest years in Galveston history. Amazingly, the entire project was carried off without a single condemnation suit, demonstrating the spirit with which Islanders approached a feat that amounted to pulling themselves up by their own bootstraps.

Today, howls of indignation arise over the resurfacing of a major street during tourist season. But the lengths to which Isle citizens were willing to go to resuscitate their beloved sandbar after the 1900 Storm proves the grit and determination lying in their hearts.

Never, never underestimate the indomitable spirit of the folks who have lived—and still live—in this historic city, one that was literally wrested from the sea.

The 1880s: Birth of the Beachfront

Galveston in 1880 was a growing community in the state of Texas and the financial hub of the opening Southwest. The Confederacy's Stars and Bars were replaced by the American flag in 1865, and during those fifteen years, trade unions were established, a street railway system begun, the Tremont Opera House opened, and the first historical society in the state formed. The Galveston Cotton Exchange opened, and the Mallory Line began steamship service between Galveston and the East Coast. Railway service was expanding, and the first telephone in Texas was installed at the *Galveston Daily News* in 1878. Between 1880 and 1881 the Island was visited by former President Ulysses S. Grant and President Benjamin Harrison. Galveston's public school system opened.

But even as Galveston's "conventional" economy was booming, there were also those who recognized the call of the sea, the charm of the beaches, and the attraction of an island city. And so, the business of tourism was born.

According to *Galveston: A History* by David McComb:

Within a month after the City Company began to sell lots in 1838, President of the Republic Sam Houston, with some of the members of Texas' congress, took an excursion ride to Galveston

The Electric Pavilion, a two-story beach resort, featured new-fangled bright lights and quickly became a major Island attraction.
—Courtesy the Rosenberg Library

from the young nation's capital on Buffalo Bayou. The seat of government at the time was none too comfortable, and they probably needed a vacation. Littleton Fowler, a Methodist minister, accompanied them, to his regret. On the boat he saw "great men in high life." They stripped to their underwear in view of the shocked preacher. "Their Bacchanalian revels and bloodcurdling profanity made the pleasure boat a floating hell," he recorded. It was too much for the delicate preacher, and he physically collapsed after the trip.

Just before Christmas that same year, a young woman and her four children visited in Galveston, where they rode in a wagon, pulled by a team of horses, to the beach. Joyfully, they gathered treasured seashells. A British diplomat discovered sand dollars while on our beach and collected them, although he complained that they were brittle and easily broken. In 1875 another visitor, though delighted by the beach, wrote in his diary that he "couldn't get a cigar or a cocktail under twenty-five cents and there was very little 'proof' in the whisky or 'Spanish' in the cigar. But there was the beach—superbly magnificent!"

Oddly enough, few of the beachfront's initial visitors actually bathed in the warm Gulf waters, the problem being, "what to wear?" McComb explores this uniquely Victorian dilemma:

> In the 19th century, few bathers were seen in bathing suits, which were not a common item of apparel. In fact, during the Civil War, the city had an ordinance prohibiting nude bathing between sunrise and sunset. "The city changed the ordinance in 1869, 1870, 1876 and 1877 as violations continued. The law of 1877 prohibited bathing in the Gulf between 16th Street and 27th Street from 4 a.m. to 10 p.m., . . . unless clothed in a costume sufficient to cover the body from neck to knee, arms excepted."
>
> The *Galveston Daily News* in 1869 described how to make a bathing suit. "Male and female styles were the same. It was best, according to the newspaper, to use twilled flannel, moreen or serge. Stiff wool was preferred because they did not cling as much as other fabrics when wet. . . . The blouse was made like a sack with separate trousers full over the hips and loose at the ankles. A full skirt could be worn if desired. . . . The hair could be protected with an oilskin cap—a large round bag with a pull string along the edge.

McComb notes that the result was not flattering, and that most women getting out of the Gulf in their soggy clothes "looked much the worse for wear as the wet garments hung closely to their forms."

Through the next twenty years, numerous arrests were made for boys bathing in the nude, and police officers often gathered up the clothes on the beach and awaited their collection at the police station, where the boys were fined for swimming *au naturel*. A story notes that in 1873 a mixed group of men and women were swimming at the beach while their horse (and wagon) were parked on the sand above them. The animal, feeling deserted, decided to walk home and left with the wagon and all their clothes. You can only imagine their predicament.

Despite such mishaps, the beach became more popular; streetcars began regular service to the Gulf shore in 1877, giving all classes of people access to the beach all day. Beachwear, too, evolved from the somber, soggy habits of the mid-1800s, making a dip in the Gulf a pleasure for both the bather and the spectator—and thus, Galveston's chief attraction came into its own, as today thousands of people yearly flock to enjoy the surf and sun on our Island.

One of the first to take notice of the value of attracting visitors to the Island was the Galveston Surf Bathing Company, chartered in 1881 to build bathhouses between 10th and 30th streets. Following closely, the Galveston City Railway Company built the Galveston Pavilion at 21st Street and Avenue Q. As McComb records, "The Street Car Company hoped to increase patronage by placing this two-story resort on the beach. Designed by Nicholas J. Clayton, the most important architect of the Island City, the Pavilion boasted 16,000 square feet of unobstructed floor space made possible by four steel arches which carried the load of the wooden structure."

Electric lights shone from this building, a first in Texas. The lighting was its biggest attraction—electric lighting being such a novelty at this time—and the Railway Company quickly capitalized, calling the resort the "Electric Pavilion." People paid to see it; they paid to use the bathhouse; and they paid to ride the trolley there and back. At the Pavilion, shows and dancing areas provided space for 5,000 participants and were very popular. In July 1882 a number of lawyers held a meeting at the Electric Pavilion and organized the Texas Bar Association, in what had to be the granddaddy of Galveston's convention business.

The new-fangled bright lights shone on Galveston Beach but briefly; the Electric Pavilion caught fire at 2 A.M. on August 1, 1883, and it burned to the ground in twenty-five minutes.

It took three years from the time the *Galveston Daily News* proposed a hotel on the Gulf, with galleries to take advantage of the sea breezes, for the president of the streetcar company to lead a public subscription drive to finance construction of the $260,000 Beach Hotel. Again, Nicholas Clayton was called upon to design the building. Clayton's plans showed the hotel to be supported by 300 cedar piles driven into the sand. Rising three stories high, it would offer 200 rooms and eighteen-foot verandas. "It was color-ful," McComb informs us. "The building itself was mauve, the eaves were trimmed in a golden green, and the roof had an octag-onal dome painted in large red and white stripes . . . It gave the impression of three pavilions with gables and ornate grillwork pushed together to form an enormous "E" configuration. It had a dining room, gentlemen's parlor and reading room, saloon, grand staircase, electric and gas lighting, and water tanks in the dome. It opened July 4, 1883, after a grand celebration the night before."

The Beach Hotel was the place to be for Galveston society. In the summertime, the lovely, wide front lawn was a beehive of activity. With music in the background, the crowd was enthralled by the sure-footed high-wire walkers (the equivalent, I guess, to 1990s bungee jumpers). As soon as it was dark, glorious fire-works reached into the night sky, and with a cacophony of booms and hisses, the brilliant sparks slowly floated downward, returning to their reflections in the water. As a matter of fact, the band offered concerts every night except Wednesday.

And here we are, at the dawn of a new century. Galveston's baby tourism business has grown up. Our visitors now number in the hundreds of thousands. Our attractions are as fine and interesting as you will find anywhere. But one thing has remained the same: We still love to gather our families together in the cool of a summer's evening to catch the slightest breeze, and relax, listen to a summer band concert, and share a moment in common with our forebears in simply sitting back and enjoy-ing our special island home.

Four lovely young ladies vied for a silver trophy that was to be presented to the winner of the "Most Perfect Back" contest, as recorded in this photo by Marino Mihovil, Sr.

—Courtesy Robert John Mihovil

From Parading Butchers to Splash Day, Islanders Love a Party

Galvestonians, being a prosperous and pleasure-loving people, have always enjoyed their festival days and unique contests. In the mid- to late 1850s, popular celebrations included July 4th; May Day, honoring the Goddess of Flowers (and, of course, the lovely young ladies of the community); Election Day; Christmas; and even a festival to salute the new fire engine house—any excuse for a celebration. There were Mardi Gras parades, some of them costing $10,000 or more, and circus parades. New Year's Day saw the "Parade of Butchers," when the Island's butchers donned masks and marched in formation from saloon to saloon.

The early 1900s saw the arrival of the "Cotton Carnival," with parades, balls, and exciting auto races on the beach. Established to attract planters and cotton-industry big shots, its purpose was strictly business. On the other hand, there was the Neptune Festival, which was organized strictly for fun and to promote tourism; it advertised six days of pleasure and six nights of mirth.

Interestingly, the 1930s saw perhaps the most creative contests ever presented on the Island. One was a part of Splash Day (more on that one later) and was named the "Glamburger Girl No. 1 Carhop Queen Contest." Carhops, carrying hamburgers and drinks on trays held high above their heads, raced for the finish line at Murdoch's Pier, hoping they would not spill anything.

Another not very well known but nonetheless innovative contest capitalized on the Island's healthy climate. This was billed as the "Hay Fever King and Queen Contest." Hay fever sufferers entered from all over the country, with the Associated Press noting that "hay fever is achieving social distinction" in Galveston. Winners of the contest were presented crowns adorned with ragweed. Over the life of the event, Walt Disney gave permission for Sneezy the Dwarf to be the official mascot. Various displays were held around town featuring collections of ragweeds, handkerchiefs, and other whimsical items.

In 1937 Dr. Marino Mihovil, a local chiropractor, organized the "Most Perfect Back" contest. It was held at Menard Park, in conjunction with the final session of the Texas Chiropractic Association convention. Twenty-seven young ladies from all over the state competed for $300 and a silver trophy. The entrants appeared in backless formal evening dress. Judging was based on general physical health, perfect back formation, and posture.

The Most Perfect Back contest drew national newspaper coverage, and newsreel cameramen representing Paramount, Pathé, and Universal studios filmed the event for distribution in movie theaters nationwide. Drawing 10,000 spectators, it was at the time perhaps the largest crowd ever to fill Menard Park. The music was provided by the Isle's own Municipal Band, today's Galveston Beach Band.

And then there was Splash Day.

Originated in 1916 by the manager of the Galvez Hotel, Splash Day was one of Galveston's most famous celebrations, heralding the opening of the beaches for summer.

One of the early Splash Day events was the Bathing Girl Revue, beginning in 1920. Later named the International Pageant of Pulchritude, this event was the forerunner of today's Miss Universe Pageant. Competition was intense—a young Dorothy Lamour entered the Bathing Girl Revue and was unsuccessful in her bid for the crown and the $2,500 cash prize! However, she went on to Hollywood and starred with Bob Hope and Bing Crosby in their famed "Road" movies. (One wonders, if Miss Lamour had won that early beauty contest, whether "The Road To Galveston" might have been added to that string of 1940s hits!)

In 1929 Splash Day and the pageant made quite a splash. Twenty-seven special trains arrived in Galveston, and the Santa Fe Railroad added extra cars to its trains. Miss Oklahoma's arrival by airplane was so exciting that she was given a parade through downtown Galveston.

Even though the young ladies were chaperoned, there were protesters who decried the contests as "a destruction to all sense of modesty." According to David McComb, the event most probably received a great deal of publicity after Bishop Brendan Byrne's comment that it was "an uncouth, vulgar display. I cannot see how any self-respecting or decent young lady would enter such a contest."

Splash Day was eventually a victim of its own popularity, driven out of business in 1965 by crowd-control problems.

But Galveston and Galvestonians still like a good party. The year 1974 saw Islanders dress up at Christmastime in nineteenth-century garb and gather on the newly restored Strand for a modest block party, "Dickens Evening on the Strand." Now a citywide celebration featuring food, beer, hot cider, roasted chestnuts, banana bread, and street entertainment, "Dickens," as most people simply call it, has become a focal point of community spirit. And Mardi Gras, revived in 1985 after dying out during World War II, draws half a million revelers to the Island to cheer on the big Grand Night Parade and scramble for beads and doubloons tossed from the colorful-to-the-point-of-gaudiness floats.

Galvestonians are a laid-back people; offer them a gold-tinged sunset over West Bay or a quiet, contemplative walk along the high-tide line, and they're more than happy.

But that doesn't mean they don't like to party down, given half a chance!

The Bay Froze, the Snow Drifted, but Isle Streetcars Rolled On

As hot as Galveston summers tend to be, it's hard to imagine a time when snowplows had to be called on to deal with the aftermath of a blizzard—but it's true. And the story goes like this:

In 1895 Galveston Island was hit by a severe winter storm. If you can believe it, the bay froze, and numbed fish floated in the surf. Plumbers working on frozen pipes became heroes. And when the storm dumped fourteen inches—that's right, one foot and two inches—of snow on the Island, the Galveston streetcars had to have snowplows affixed to their front ends to help clear the streets. (Don't you wonder where snowplows were found in this part of the world?)

Streetcars had been serving Galveston since 1868, when the Galveston City Railroad began operations with mule-drawn cars. In 1891 electricity, the new urban power source, was applied to some of the streetcars—but not all of them. Some forty-three mule cars were still operating at the time of the great snowstorm. Can't you just picture these mule-drawn carts struggling through the snowy streets?

And another trolley story: Ashton Villa, at 24th and Broadway, was the home of James Brown and his family. Built in 1859, it was one of the first brick mansions in Texas. It was even reputed to have a ghost, Miss Bettie Brown, the daughter of the builder, who long after her death could still be heard playing the piano in the Gold Room.

"She was known to have had a chronic bronchial cough loud enough to startle the streetcar mules, out on the street. Amused contemporaries had gathered to witness the plodding animals awaken with a surprised 'hee-haw!' and bolt for the turntable two blocks away," wrote Pete Fredriksen for the magazine *InBetween*.

Gradually, the mule cars were retired, and in 1905 the trolley system was completely electrified. In 1930 bus lines began to replace trolleys, and in 1938 the streetcar operation was retired.

But here we are in the twenty-first century—sixty years later—and again enjoying a nostalgic trolley ride. Today's Galveston trolleys, some red and some green, may not be powered by overhead electric lines like the old ones, but the sounds are the same as they clatter and grind down the tracks, brakes screeching on the curves, the motorman sounding his distinctive, high-pitched warning whistle. A soft, warm wind brushes your face as you gaze out the open window while the trolley winds its way through the heart of the city. Then, as the car turns the corner onto the Seawall, you can feel the fresh, cooling Gulf breezes. Take a trolley ride—you'll feel like you have stepped back in time to slower, gentler days on Galveston Island.

Until their retirement in 1905, mule-drawn streetcars served Galveston for 125 years.

—Courtesy the Rosenberg Library

Auto's Advent Rattled Isle into Twentieth Century

For almost one hundred years, the automobile has been on Galveston Island. Seth Mabry Morris of the medical school reputedly owned the first automobile in Galveston, a 1902 Oldsmobile, and the first advertisements for autos appeared in 1903. Despite the fact that drivers were limited to the Island, cars became popular. One driving enthusiast said, "This makes no difference to me, because I can find plenty of sport driving in town and on the beach with my car." Excursions to San Luis Pass, racing over the sand, and a maiden trip to Houston in 1909, enhanced Islanders' growing love affair with the automobile. By the end of 1909, Galveston had three garages and 145 cars on the streets.

"The city imposed driving on the right hand side of the road in 1907, license plates in 1908, a 10-mile-per-hour speed limit in 1910, and head- and taillights in 1911," reports David McComb. The first streetlight was installed at 23rd Street and Seawall Boulevard in 1914.

By 1917 the trend was obvious. Motor trucks were taking the place of mules and wagons, cars replaced horses, and new stories surfaced. McComb quotes Judge O. B. Wigley, who avowed that "a speedometer was unnecessary for the Model T: At 10 miles per hour the lamps rattled, at 20 miles per hour the fenders rattled, at 30 miles per hour the windshield rattled, and faster than that your bones rattled."

Because of the popularity of the auto, there was a demand for better roads and, of course, a bridge to the mainland. In 1912 the railroads built a causeway to the mainland. Replicating a viaduct along the Florida Keys, twenty-eight concrete arches with seventy-foot spans allowed room for two railroads, the Interurban tracks, a thirty-inch water main, and a nineteen-foot roadway for autos. When the causeway opened, Gov. Oscar B. Colquitt led a line of 1,500 cars and cut a ribbon in the middle of the causeway. It was an exciting day, celebrated with shrieking

The sport of auto racing on the hard-packed sand beaches drew large, enthusiastic crowds in the early 1900s.

–Courtesy the Rosenberg Library

whistles, brilliant fireworks, too many speeches, and a ball at the Galvez Hotel.

Another causeway, just for cars, opened in 1938, and a three-and-a-half-fold increase in traffic made a third causeway necessary. The newest causeway opened in 1961 and rose seventy-two feet above the water, obviating the need for a drawbridge, which could delay traffic. The 1938 causeway was refurbished and raised to the same level of the new one and in 1964 was reopened. The 1912 causeway has long been closed to auto traffic but still provides the only rail link between the mainland and the Isle.

As we face a new century, a fourth causeway is a distinct possibility. The romance and history of this beautiful island have attracted hundreds of thousands of visitors whose motorized vehicles crowd the existing roadways as they flock to our Island to share for a day . . . a week . . . or a month . . . the splendor of our life, beginning with the sun rising gloriously out of the Gulf, the day-long swash of the sea caressing the sand, ending with a radiant sunset that slowly and silently fades into comforting darkness.

Isle Aviation Takes Off with New Airport, "Wrong-Way" Corrigan

In 1912 Galvestonians were astounded by the amazing news that the first airmail flight from Galveston to La Marque had been accomplished. At this time, Galveston didn't have an airport, only a dirt landing strip in a field on the south side of Offatt's Bayou. In 1932, however, many were present at the opening of the brand-new Galveston Municipal Airport, offering not only airmail but passenger service. Only the bravest of the brave, with enough money, availed themselves of this service.

In 1938 Galveston captured headlines when a native son made a nonstop flight across the ocean. Most of you remember the young pilot who filed a flight plan from New York to California . . . and ended up in Ireland. That young, red-headed, freckle-faced Irishman, Douglas Corrigan, went down in the history books as "Wrong-Way Corrigan."

The government had clamped down on flights across the Atlantic because too many had lost their lives trying to duplicate Lindbergh's flight. So Corrigan filed a flight plan for California, but instead flew his rickety Curtiss Robin monoplane across the Atlantic to Ireland. Questioned by authorities, Corrigan claimed his compass had been defective and said simply, "I went the wrong way."

However the federal regulators may have regarded his trip, Corrigan was a media hero, and Isle Mayor Adrian Levy invited him to visit his old hometown. His visit was not a smashing success. When presented with a wristwatch, he said he already had several, and when he was escorted to the Guild Building at 21st and Market to see a plaque that had been installed in one of the rooms proclaiming it to be the room where Corrigan was born, he announced with visible annoyance that he was born in the John Sealy Hospital, not the Guild Building. Corrigan, it is also said, was unhappy that a particular beer company was his sponsor. His behavior squelched any excitement about his visit and any talk about honoring him by naming the new municipal airport Corrigan Airport.

In 1942 our airport became an army air force base and was called Scholes Field (pronounced, by the way, "Skoals," not "Shoals") in honor of the airport manager—and a busy base it was. Fort Crockett, on Seawall, was the army base, and the Crash Basin (which I always thought might have had a frightening connection with airplanes crashing into it) was really just a small body of water connected to Offatt's Bayou west of the airport, so named because crash boats trained there during World War II.

Of interest, and not generally known, is Col. Charles "Lucky Lindy" Lindbergh's unscheduled landing here in Galveston on April 13, 1944. On his way from the East Coast to the West Coast, and then on to the Pacific theater of war, his chart called for a refueling stop at the navy base at Hitchcock. As he flew over the area, he found a large grass fire burning on the windward side of the field and smoke covering most of the landing area. By radio he was told that even if he could land, this was not a regular airfield, but a blimp base. They didn't have any 100-octane aviation gasoline and they suggested he head for the Galveston army air base. After circling, he landed, refueled, checked the weather, cleared, and took off.

I have the feeling this man would have appreciated our island, for just three days earlier, he was in Florida and recorded these thoughts about a party he had attended: "For a few minutes I was sitting in a chair with a view of the bay and the rising moon. Everything was so beautiful outside, and because it was a party and they were entertaining me, they had not the slightest realization of what was out there just beyond their windows. I would have given anything to go out alone for just a quarter of an hour."

And so, with that thought, I leave you. Look out beyond your windows and take in the beautiful moments you have here on historic, romantic Galveston Island.

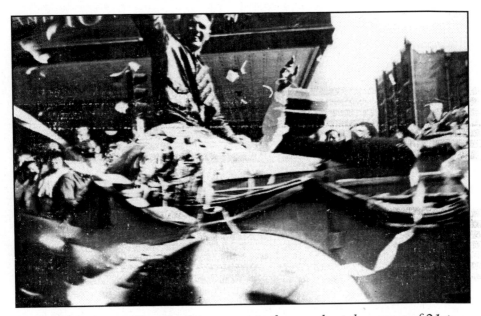

In 1938 Wrong-Way Corrigan waves to the crowds at the corner of 21st and Postoffice during a tickertape parade in his honor.
—Marino M. Mihovil, Jr. (Father of photographer
Robert John Mihovil, Marino Junior took the picture when
he was seven years old, using an ordinary dollar box camera.)

Of Nickel Ice Cream, Soda Fizzes, and Warm Isle Evenings

Remember when this was a popular song—"The sweetest girl I ever saw was sipping soda through a straw"? Well, on Galveston Island you might have heard, "The neatest guy I ever saw was serving sodas with a straw." During the "good ole days," Galveston boasted over fifty drugstore soda fountains and drive-in eateries. And the soda jerks and carhops were usually young men!

On warm summer days, the thought of a tall root beer float bubbling with vanilla ice cream in a frosted mug is a cooling memory. They were once available for just 5 cents at Kniexley's. Or remember the W&S at 6th and Seawall, where they made their own ice cream and candy? The carhops were all young boys who worked not for a salary, but just for tips. A nickel would buy an ice cream cone, a milk shake, or a root beer; a Coney hot dog with chili and warm melted cheese in a bun was 6 cents; and a super hamburger, a dime. At those prices, the boys had to wait on a lot of customers to earn enough tip money to buy a bicycle, go to a movie, or take a pretty girl out on a date. Boys coveted these summer jobs, and, of course, the owners looked for young men from large families, as moms, dads, aunts, uncles, grandparents, sisters, brothers and cousins would all come to the place where their favorite relative worked. These were choice jobs, and the young boys grew up to become successful Galveston businessmen—one even became the mayor of Galveston.

Remember the soda fizz? Sweet and cold, and just 5 cents. You bought one even if it meant you had to walk home from a movie in town, because you spent the 4 cents car fare, plus a penny more, for that refreshing fizz.

On Sundays, on the way home from church, the family would stop to buy Sunday dinner's dessert: A gallon of the very best homemade ice cream, made with pure cream, for just one dollar. Who can ever forget the Triple Dip; J & R Ice Cream; the Ice Company on Avenue K; and the roasted, salted peanuts at Debuoy's? And way down at the West End, the Silver Bell at 35th and Broadway; or Depen's, where Gaido's is today, at 39th and Seawall.

The Star Drug Store was the oldest Island soda fountain, still serving loyal customers in the 1990s.

– Robert John Mihovil

There was a wealth of drugstores run by the town's most prominent citizens: Cardray's, Termini's, Williamson's. The Williamson brothers worked with their dad and have stayed in the business ever since—although they no longer have soda fountains.

How times have changed—no more soda fountains in drugstores. We have our fat and cholesterol to worry about; we want fat-free ice milk or yogurt. And if we do decide to cast care aside and indulge ourselves, we will probably pay more than a dollar and a half for a nickel cone!

Wartime: Soldiers, Sweethearts, Carousels, and Moonlit Beaches

As America became involved in World War II, Galveston Island became a military rest and recreation center for servicemen stationed in the area. Fresh-faced recruits wearing crisp new uniforms flocked to Galveston by the thousands, arriving in buses, trucks, trains, and cars. They joyfully burst into town seeking relief from rigorous military training. Additionally, soldiers were stationed at Camp Wallace in Hitchcock and in Galveston at Fort Crockett. The navy had men stationed on Pelican Island, while the Galvez Hotel was converted into Coast Guard barracks. Scholes Airfield was home to twenty-five B-17 bombers, and at one point the *Galveston Daily News* ran a paragraph asking the patience of West End residents as the huge, four-engine "Flying Fortresses" throbbed just overhead, noting that the training their crews received in Galveston was vital to the war effort.

Throngs of soldiers, sailors, and marines strolled along the Seawall, enjoying the warm sun, soft Gulf breezes, and pretty girls. Red, pink, and white oleanders bloomed in all their glory, seagulls wheeled and squawked overhead, and gentle waves lapped the sand. Along the strip, generally between 25th and 21st streets, a kalcidoscope of amusements and entertainment beckoned the uniformed crowds. There was an enormous carousel at 25th Street, with life-sized racing horses, its music blending with the racket of shooting galleries and midway games next door. The Mountain Speedway roller coaster behind the Buccaneer Hotel on 22nd Street roared up and down and round and round; and a giant Ferris wheel swung riders high into the sky. The glittering Balinese Room offered Hollywood entertainers and gambling in its aerie perched out over the surf at 21st Street. Seafood restaurants abounded, every shop and bar offered slot machines and tip books, and Murdoch's Pier had swimming, refreshments, and beauty contests. It was paradise on earth.

City officials required that after dark, automobiles use only parking lights along Seawall Boulevard and for five blocks from the beach, while no cars at all would be allowed on the sand.

One Victory Bond and stamp campaign started with a band concert at Menard Park and the hanging in effigy of Adolph Hitler. A parade of jeeps with soldiers from Fort Crockett and Camp Wallace drove up, and a machine gun unit climbed up the roof of the E. S. Levy & Co. building.

Drives were organized to collect tin cans, waste fats, and rubber goods. Housewives saved leftover grease in one-pound cans and sold it to local meat markets for 4 cents per pound. The butchers then sold the grease to the nearest soap-making plant. Citizens donated binoculars to the cause, and every bit of scrap metal on the Island was given to the war effort (latter-day Isle historian and then–"Mayor of Fairville" Maury Darst was pictured in a 1942 issue of the *Daily News*—all of seven years old—proudly displaying a pile of scrap he had collected).

As the war progressed and the threat of submarine activities increased, Fort Crockett officers banned the public from most of the beaches, day or night. They warned that armed patrols with orders to shoot would be on duty. Still, a few small beaches and Stewart Beach remained open. Civil defense leaders staged a mock attack to keep their volunteers alert and ready for action. There were simulated injuries, and the Red Cross participated, carrying off the splinted and bandaged "victims." Doctors and nurses examined them, and when the all-clear signal sounded, the show was over and everybody went home feeling the exercise was a great success.

At last, on August 15, 1945, the welcome news arrived—Japan had surrendered; the long war was finally over. In a recorded radio message, Emperor Hirohito called upon the Japanese people to "bear the unbearable" and lay down their arms.

On the Isle, jubilant office workers threw streams of tickertape from their windows while youngsters hanged Tojo in effigy. Merchant seamen in port from Great Britain and Norway gathered at the British and Allied Merchant Navy Club. A spontaneous and constant party swept through the city as people in cars, on bikes, or afoot greeted each other with shouts and jubilant honks on their car horns. There were no strangers; everyone was a fellow American, shaking hands with every other fellow American he met. Church bells mingled with laughter and all the other sounds of giddy celebration in a joyous symphony that had no score but was titled "Peace On Earth."

V-J Day meant the end of rationing of gasoline and canned goods, and the prayers for peace in the world were answered. Citizens here gave thanks, bade farewell to the soldiers, sailors, marines, and airmen who had thronged the town "for the duration," then prepared to return to the gentle ebb and flow of peacetime life in the Island City.

During World War II, soldiers stationed at Fort Crockett protected the Gulf Coast with a disappearing seacoast gun.

—Courtesy National Archives

Galveston's Summer of '42:
Lonely GIs Ashore, U-Boats Offshore

Summer comes, and summer goes—too fast, for most of us. For some reason, it is the passage of summers more than any other season that serves as a constant reminder of time's relentless flight. We look back at summers spent at Grandma's, summers at camp, the summer breaks in our school years. Today, we're going to pull one long-past summer off the shelf and live it again: The summer of 1942—just yesterday to some of us, almost ancient history to others.

It was wartime, a time that changed the face of Galveston. Young men suddenly found their lives altered—students one day, soldiers the next. They were stationed far from home, at places like Camp Wallace in Hitchcock or in Galveston at Fort Crockett. Weekend passes found them strolling the Galveston Seawall, watching the surf rolling in—and of course, the girls, always an attraction all over the world.

But Galveston civilians did their part, as well. A well-known poster featured a combat GI dashing into battle while a young woman defense worker stood stoically in the background. "The girl he left behind is still behind him now," read its inspiring message.

Times were not easy. Milk was rationed. Sugar was rationed. Meat was rationed, and so were other items such as ketchup and gasoline. But those concerns were small compared to the overwhelming worry for the safety of loved ones.

Do you remember the prices back then? Let me list some for you: Women's swimsuits, $1.98. Rayon hose, 25 cents. Sixteen-inch push mower (muscle-powered!), $18.95. Diapers, $1.79 a dozen. Women's sport shoes, $1.99. Summer dress, $5.95.

And food! Onions, three pounds for 10 cents. Potatoes, ten pounds for 45 cents. Oranges, 25 cents a dozen. Butter, 45 cents a pound, if you could get it—it was rationed. And the bread to put it on, 11 cents a loaf.

Oh, and just listen to these meat prices: Bacon, 32 cents a pound. Rib roast, 29 cents a pound. Dressed fryers, 39 cents a pound. Veal, just 19 cents a pound.

German U-boat-536 offshore . . . lights out onshore.
—Courtesy First Officer Wolfgang VonBartenwerffer

For party time, Seagram's 7-Crown Whiskey was just $3.09 a quart. And for the next morning, you could buy 100 Bayer Aspirin tablets for 39 cents.

It all sounds so cheap in today's dollars. But remember—a GI made just twenty-one dollars a month!

People who lived in Galveston that summer will remember the regular nighttime blackouts on Seawall Boulevard. It was against the law to turn on so much as a flashlight; even a match light for a cigarette could give the German ships and submarines out in the Gulf something to aim at. Shades had to be drawn at home, and there were volunteer civilian air raid wardens on every block to warn you if any light showed.

Although the Boulevard was black as pitch, the cool evening breezes beckoned as always, and even in the dark many people walked quietly and listened to the haunting sounds of the surf washing the sands at the foot of the protective Seawall.

The ever-present lure of the sea: Summer after summer, in war as well as in peacetime, some things never change.

When People Rode Trains, They Rode Them to Galveston

Here on Galveston Island we've become accustomed to the sounds that surround us: the Gulf washing the sands, the cries of the sea birds—and not too very long ago, the puffing of steam engines, the clickity-clack of lumbering railcars, and the lonesome wail of whistles as the trains headed for the Galveston Union Station.

In 1836, three years before Galveston was officially incorporated as a city, a railroad charter was issued. But not until seventeen years later, at the Port of Galveston, was the first train in Galveston, the "General Sherman," put into service. Eventually, in 1873, the Gulf, Colorado and Santa Fe Railroad later became the Atchison, Topeka and Santa Fe. (I wonder if "Chattanooga Choo-Choo" Glenn Miller's saxophone player, Tex Beneke, told him about that train?)

A number of well-known, "name" trains once called at Union Station, on 25th Street at the head of Strand, during the heyday of passenger train travel. Redcaps scurried to and from the train sheds. Taxicabs anxiously awaited fares, and streetcars and buses were nearby. Waitresses known as the "Harvey Girls," at the Fred Harvey House, stood ready to serve travelers or local residents, who often ate in the spacious restaurant. By 1932 Galveston boasted it could connect to a network of 18,000 miles of track.

The Santa Fe's Sunshine Special arrived daily from St. Louis, offering full sleeping-car accommodations, a dining car, and chair cars. Later, the name was changed to the Texas Eagle, and it made connections in Houston to the Valley. Eagle service for Baton Rouge and New Orleans ended in 1954. The Missouri, Kansas and Texas' Katy Flyer traveled the tracks until 1942. Remember the Texas Chief? Headquartered in Galveston, the Chief became a name train in the late 1940s with complete service including lounges, chair cars, a diner, Pullman, and roomettes as it headed north to Chicago. The Ranger, until 1957, arrived at midmorning and departed in early evening, destination Oklahoma City. The California Special ran between Galveston, Houston, Temple, Lubbock, and points west; it

Engine 555 steams eastward, tooting its whistle to announce its arrival at Galveston's Union Station.

—Robert John Mihovil

stopped operating in the early 1930s. And a nameless train, known only as "the Beaumont Train," had to be ferried across the Galveston Channel and operated until 1942.

When the Texas Eagle stopped running in 1954, passenger service into and out of the city essentially ended. Union Station became known simply as the Santa Fe Passenger Station, and later, after renovation, was renamed Shearn Moody Plaza.

Today, this is where the legend, lore, and legacy of Texas railroading comes to life. The Galveston Island Railroad Museum houses the largest collection of restored rail cars and locomotives in the Southwest. Forty-two unique pieces of rail equipment, including steam and diesel locomotives, Pullman passenger cars, and turn-of-the-century freight cars now await crowds of visitors at the station platform, as they once awaited rushing passengers bound for "points elsewhere."

The wail of the whistle and the conductor's urgent "Booooard!" may be long gone, but the trains are still here—a grandly scaled still life of bygone times on a proud and bustling Galveston Island.

Even Strong Hearts Got Weak-Kneed on the Mountain Speedway

Galvestonians have always been fascinated by cars and boats and planes and trains. We even have museums in honor of each of these modes of transportation.

The first automobile owners got their thrills by racing cars on the hard-packed sand of the beach. And for the auto-less, the Mountain Speedway roller coaster, which stood at 22nd and Avenue P½, could give as many thrills as any Texas Cyclone— and even a few spills. "A familiar landmark for many years," wrote Maury Darst, "the white structure loomed over the rooftops of buildings that surrounded it. Only the Galvez and Buccaneer hotels outclassed the wooden frame for height.

"At times," continued Darst, "crowds stood in long lines for a chance to climb into one of the wooden cars for an evening's spin around the track. As the car clattered up the initial incline, riders could capture a breathtaking view of Galveston twinkling in the summer sky." When the car finally reached the summit, only the very brave would stand up as it plunged over the arc on its downward dash. Often, if the wind was blowing steadily from the north, it was said you could even feel the structure sway to and fro, just before the car plummeted down toward what seemed oblivion. The first drop only barely prepared you for the second race toward ground zero.

As the car hurtled around the track, you could smell the wooden brakes, or arresters, controlling its headlong rush. Darst captured the experience:

> An operator, standing near the ticket counter, operated all the braking systems of the beachfront attraction. A number of youthful roller coaster buffs would often journey to Houston to ride a similar machine on South Main in Houston, but many said the Galveston ride was better, more exciting. Rumors flew that it was condemned.
>
> "Ride it anyway," someone said.
>
> "Makes it even more exciting," another exclaimed.
>
> "Gee, fellows, I dunno. I don't have any life insurance," one meek-hearted youngster said, his hands trembling. "I'll wait 'til you get back."
>
> Another declared, "My mom told me if I rode that thing, and she found out, I was gonna get it."
>
> "I rode it only once," said a native Galvestonian nearing his eighty-fifth birthday. And the stories go on.
>
> Some seasons, the Mountain Speedway opened late. It was often closed for repairs. Finally, after the 1957 season, few cars went up the incline and sped around the twisting, narrow curves.
>
> "One fellow even fell out of a car. It didn't kill him, but you should have seen the operator's face when the car came back empty!" one Galvestonian said.

Finally, it was torn down—and just in time, for about a year later a tornado spawned by Hurricane Carla rumbled across the area where the roller coaster once stood. Some years later, construction began on the Turner Geriatric Center, which today occupies the site. Other adjoining structures, some of which also carved a niche in Galveston's history, were also bulldozed.

No markers or monuments mark the site of the Mountain Speedway, but its hellbent-for-leather rush and its lovely, if brief, vistas of sea, sand, and sky live on in the memories of those who once were young and carefree on Galveston Island.

Glittering in the night, the Mountain Speedway beckoned those seeking a thrilling ride. Only the Galvez and Buccaneer hotels outclassed the Speedway for height.

—Courtesy the Rosenberg Library

1958: Slow-Dancing at the Marine Room, Utah Carl on the Motorola

In 1958 television was still a black-and-white infant. KGUL-TV of Galveston starred Western singing hero Utah Carl. Carl's theme song was "I'm Just a Wanderer of the Wasteland," and almost everyone watched his program because it was live, local, and, many said, "fascinating." On Friday nights, a giant twenty-one-inch, black-and-white Motorola broadcasting the wrestling matches from Houston, or the Pabst Blue Ribbon boxing matches from anywhere, coupled with a bowl of popcorn and a Coke, was a great way to spend an inexpensive evening.

"However," wrote Jim Brigance in the *Galveston Daily News,* "the more adventurous may have spent 90 cents on a tag team wrestling match at Galveston's City Auditorium on 24th Street or wandered over to the Pleasure Pier, site of today's Flagship Hotel, at 25th and Seawall:

> On a balmy Saturday night in 1958, you could be a big spender, paying your 50 cents to enter the pier and another $1.25 to dance the night away at the Pier's Marine Room.
>
> Those not up to the rhythms of the McCoy Brothers Orchestra could listen to the surf roaring beneath the pier, and watch water clowns, beautiful girls, and diving champs stage spectacular shows of derring-do. A day at the beach, especially during the Splash Days, was different in 1958. Women's bathing suits left a lot more to the imagination than the dots and dashes worn by the free-spirited women of today. And you could buy one at Levy's for $6.00. (Don't laugh—that was a fairly high price, considering a woman could buy two pairs of shorts for 77 cents.) Or you could haul your new barbecue pit to the beach—the one that you paid $7.99 for at Weingarten's.
>
> Over the causeway, Texas City's Showboat Theater was pretty glitzy, but not nearly as lavish as the Martini or State theaters in Galveston. Drive-in theaters like the Bayou in La Marque or the Oleander in Galveston offered teen-agers a place to go where the automobile became a steel bunker against the world, with only outdoor movies permitted to intrude through the windshield.
>
> In the Galveston of 1958, most were unfamiliar with Oriental

The Pleasure Pier at Seawall and 25th Street lured big spenders who would pay $1.25 to dance the night away at the Marine Room.
                                        –Courtesy the Rosenberg Library

food. But the ongoing civil war in French Indochina—Vietnam—changed all that. Now Asian restaurants are everywhere. Back then, you had a choice of drive-in hamburgers, deep-fried seafood and chicken, or Mom's liver and onions. Bostick's Cafe in La Marque offered traditional fried specialties, as did the Golden Greek in Galveston or the Seaview and Seawall restaurants.

In the 1950s nobody had ever heard of cholesterol, or of no-smoking sections in public places. Russia had orbited Sputnik, but putting a man in space was still three years off. Houston's space center was still a cow pasture, and NASA was still spelled with a "C."

Luby's Cafeteria may have been the closest thing to Mom's home-cooked meals, assuming Mom was a good cook. For 77 cents you could dine on chicken pot pie, potatoes, peas, salad, rolls, and a grape punch drink.

Times have changed, and changed greatly. In today's over-priced, fuel-injected, microprocessed society, it's tempting to wish ourselves back in the simpler times of the fifties.

But really, now—would you want to have to watch your Indiana Jones videos on that twenty-one-inch, black-and-white Motorola?

Tropic Isle Proves Poor Retirement Home for Geriatric Lobster

In the year 1832, in the cold, deep waters of the Atlantic Ocean off the coast of South Carolina, a baby lobster took his first swim. For 154 years, he roamed the sea, outliving most of his relatives, until one day he wandered into a lobster trap and was hauled aboard a fishing boat. The fisherman had a great catch that day and did not notice the twenty-two-pound lobster, with claws twelve inches long and four inches wide, when he delivered his cargo to the market. When the ancient crustacean was delivered to the Red Lobster restaurant in Mesquite, Texas, and a lettered "lobster-ologist" determined his age, he was singled out for display, and a contest was held to find him a name. Fittingly, the winning name was "Conan," and the prize was—horrors!—Conan for dinner.

On Tuesday morning, May 6, 1986, a Houston radio station broadcast the story of Conan and the fact that he was to be the main course at dinner that very night. Sea-Arama Marineworld in Galveston, hearing of Conan's plight, offered a retirement home for the lobster, and the restaurant, besieged by calls from sympathetic Texans, substituted as many regular lobsters as the winners could eat and agreed to donate Conan to Sea-Arama.

By Wednesday morning, Conan had become a national celebrity. His story was carried on Houston television and radio. His tale was told in Houston, Galveston, and Dallas newspa-pers—and by midmorning had been picked up by the "Today"

John Kerivan, head curator, carefully lifts Conan to move him into his "retirement" home at Sea-Arama Marine World.

—Courtesy *The Galveston Daily News*

show, "Good Morning, America," and CNN. Calls from California, Connecticut, Arizona, and the Carolinas lit up Sea-Arama's switchboard. By Thursday his fame had spread to Australia via "Good Morning, Perth" and spread far to the north on a chain of forty Canadian radio stations. And on Friday night, no less an icon than Johnny Carson had a live lobster walk across his desk. Even the *Wall Street Journal* made mention of the *very* senior-citizen lobster on its front page.

Meanwhile, back in Texas, plans were made to transport Conan from Dallas to Galveston. The president of Pumpkin Air, a local helicopter service, had scheduled a trip to Galveston and agreed to bring the newly dubbed "Conan, the Sesquicentennial Lobster" to Scholes Field in Galveston and airlift him in a Pumpkin helicopter all the way across Stewart Road to Sea-Arama's front door. Sea-Arama curators were busily preparing a refrigerated saltwater tank with a large rock cave to become Conan's new retirement condo. Reservations were made for the park's assistant curator of fishes to fly to Dallas with a large insulated chest, loaned by Del Papa Distributing—whose usual trade was in Budweiser beer—to accompany Conan to his new home.

As preparations were being made for Conan's arrival, a redheaded baby boy was born in Clear Lake and promptly named Bernard Domenick Conan Garcia. Although he was too young to join the festivities, big brother Chris joined Galveston Mayor Jan Coggeshall as Conan was given an Isle welcome of the first order. The mayor said she was glad the hefty lobster was at the marine facility, close to other sea life. Former State Senator A. R. "Babe" Schwartz made Conan feel welcome by making him an honorary legislative lobbyist, since Texas lobbyists, he said, are known as "lobsters." A Galveston songster serenaded the lobster as he arrived, and the mayor pro-tem, two city councilmen, the fire chief, and the presidents of the Parks Board and the Beach Patrol were all in attendance.

But sadly, captivity did not agree with Conan. He died one month after his arrival at Sea-Arama. A simple ceremony was held in the garden next to the otter exhibit. Thirty or so mourners gathered there early on a rainy morning. Under a sea of black umbrellas, they listened to a few kind words for a lost friend and watched as a plain white casket was lowered into the ground. A small voice then asked plaintively, "Where is the melted butter?"

End of story? Not quite. Some three weeks after Conan's demise, another oversized lobster was rescued from the dinner table in Beaumont. Conan II, weighing in at twenty pounds and estimated to be 140 years old, was auctioned at a fund-raiser for the Juvenile Diabetes Foundation and then donated to Sea-Arama. A parade was held in Conan II's honor—he rode on a silver platter in a white stretch limousine from the restaurant to the airport. Again, a curator from Sea-Arama was there to bring him to Galveston. But alas, Conan II had been out of the water too long and expired on the silver platter.

No, there wasn't a Conan III—and Sea-Arama closed in 1986. But the original Conan the Lobster still lies in eternal peace at the defunct marine park, under a stone bearing a small brass plaque that reads:

> Here lies a wondrous beast
> Who weighed 22 pounds at least.
> He staved off the risk
> Of becoming a bisque
> Though he would've made a Texas-sized feast.

UTMB: Tomorrow's Doctors Bloom Today in the Oleander City

Our beautiful, almost-always-sunny Island has so many treasures to discover that one might not think of a medical center as a centerpiece of local—indeed, Texas—history. But yes, the University of Texas Medical Branch on the East End is a place you won't want to miss seeing—as a spectator, not a patient, I hope!

Most of the older units, hidden away in the shadows of today's concrete-and-glass office towers and parking garages, are stucco and brick and follow a Spanish Renaissance motif, with walls in neutral shades of buff or gray with red tile roofs. The centerpiece, though, is the Ashbel Smith building—a name that will draw blank stares from most Islanders, who have always called it "Old Red."

This red-sandstone, Romanesque Revival masterpiece was designed by Galveston's great architect, Nicholas Clayton, and completed in 1891. It was, at the time, the only building designed as a medical school west of the Mississippi. When the state medical college opened in Galveston in October of that year, this single building housed the entire school.

That situation didn't last long; the medical school soon outgrew its original quarters and expanded into newer buildings. "Old Red," ravaged by hurricanes, time, obsolescence, and neglect, was by the 1970s a crumbling white elephant, practically unoccupied, with leaking roofs and pigeons nesting in the great, round operating theaters at either end—but more about that later.

You might wonder how Galveston Island was selected as the site for the state medical school. Well, a member of one of Galveston's outstanding families is due the credit for this. John Sealy, Sr., came from Pennsylvania to make his home in Galveston in 1846, soon after Texas became a state. An extremely successful businessman, Sealy was interested in the welfare of his fellow men and offered to fund construction of a hospital. As a result of that gesture, the Texas Legislature selected Galveston as the site of the new state medical school. Sealy's son, John Junior, with his sister Jennie Sealy Smith, later established the Sealy & Smith Foundation, which was created to aid the John Sealy teaching hospital.

Some ten years after John Senior arrived here, his younger

"Old Red" is noted for its red Texas-granite columns and sandstone capitals and ornamentation. In 1891 the original cost was $65,000, including the land, and a renovation 100 years later cost $6.5 million.
—Robert John Mihovil

brother George followed. Also a successful businessman, George built a palatial residence, "Open Gates," at 25th and Broadway. The family eventually gave the home, together with an endowment, to the University of Texas Medical Branch.

Oh, and as for "Old Red"?

Happily, it was restored completely in the 1980s, to serve a modern purpose as library and office space, and as a monument to the pioneers of modern medicine in Texas and the Southwest.

So go and see our medical center—you'll find "Old Red" standing proudly on Strand Street, presiding over the modern, sprawling medical complex in Galveston's East End that is today's University of Texas Medical Branch.

"Old Red" today remains firmly implanted in the memories of thousands of doctors throughout the nation—and indeed, throughout the world, as future doctors from all over the globe flock to Galveston Island and its world-renowned medical school, born and nurtured through the philanthropy of John Sealy and his heirs.

Grand Opera House's Rescue Saves More Than a Theater

"The Grand Opera House, with its marble foyer, grand staircase, and parquet floors, was an exquisite work in miniature," writes Gary Cartwright. "Any number of American cities had 'opera houses' in the late 1800s, but they were nothing grander than vaudeville houses where song-and-dance teams, acrobats and animal acts entertained." Over the years, Galveston, too, had had several opera houses, which featured some of the great performers of the world—Sarah Bernhardt in *Tosca* and *Camille*, and Edwin Booth in *Othello* and *Julius Caesar.* The great prima donna Adelina Patti, sparkling from her head to her toes with diamonds, singing arias from Verdi's *La Traviata*, was a sight to behold.

But the new Grand Opera House, completed in 1894, was the

grandest of the grand. Modeled after the opera houses in the European capitals, the "auditorium was constructed without square corners, to prevent echoes and assure perfect acoustics. Its 1,600 plush seats were arranged in a gentle curve, stepped downward toward the stage, which was equipped to accommodate any type of production—including live-animal chariot races for performances of *Ben Hur*," adds Cartwright.

A mere six years after its opening, however, the 1900 hurricane took a severe toll on the Grand. The east wall of the opera house was destroyed, and a foul-smelling slime with the consistency of axle grease covered the floors. An arabesque cupola over the west front was lost.

Still, the opera house survived, and like its home city it came back just as grandly as ever. With typical determination, the city recovered from the disastrous storm, and if anything Island life was more idyllic and more vibrant than it had been before. "The Opera House opened again in 1901 and in the seasons that followed hosted Al Jolson, Sarah Bernhardt's farewell tour, and an ensemble from the Imperial opera houses of St. Petersburg and Moscow, featuring the world's most famous ballerina, Anna Pavlova," Cartwright informs us.

By the late 1920s, however, the Island was changing. Its usual flood of immigrants decreased drastically, resulting in a dearth of Europeans, who normally would seek out more cultural entertainment, including the opera. The Grand Opera House declined slowly, first into a movie house, then a vaudeville theater, and in 1974 it was boarded up and closed . . . but not for long.

Just at this time, the preservation movement took hold in Galveston. The Galveston Cultural Arts Council volunteers organized an arts festival on the Strand and brought ballet companies and symphonies to the Island. One of the problems was finding a suitable auditorium. Betty Hilton, with the Galveston Little Theater, had visited Martini's old State Theater—once the Grand Opera House. Impressed with the acoustics, she insisted that Emily Whiteside, director of the Cultural Arts Council, go and look at the building.

"Standing in front of the old theatre," narrates Gary Cartwright, "Emily saw what looked like a granite archway concealed beneath the rotting boards of the marquee. When she

The Grand's plush seats are arranged in a gentle curve stepped down-ward toward the stage. Three tiers of boxes are decorated with red velvet curtains, and the stage curtain is a duplicate of the original curtain, first displayed in the late 1800s.

— Robert John Mihovil

peeled back the boards, she saw letters carved in the Romanesque arch. Most of them had been broken away but she could make out one word—OPERA. A ghost breathed down the back of her neck as she realized that what she had discovered was the 1894 Grand Opera House."

The Kempner Foundation and many others backed the theater's restoration. Piece by piece, as money was raised, the renovation progressed. A 1975 Houston Opera Theater performance of Benjamin Britten's *Turn of the Screw* was the first opera performed in the Grand Opera House in sixty years and kicked off the restoration of the facility—a daunting task not completed until 1986. Now the beautiful Opera House is truly a jewel in Galveston's crown.

Today, life in Galveston appears not to have changed much over the last century. As Cartwright notes, "The changes are mostly cosmetic, a dab of concrete here, a layer of track there, a hotel, a pier, an artificial beach with white sand imported from Florida . . . Quaint cottages raised on stilts sit jammed between splendiferous mansions and fields of tangled vines and fishermen's beer joints lurk in the shadows of magnificent churches." You can still find family-owned taverns and neighborhood corner grocery stores, and trolley cars patterned after the streetcars of a hundred years ago still rumble along the streets. In Cartwright's words, "The Strand sleeps most of the week, her Victorian face scrubbed and painted and waiting for the weekends." Along the waterfront, a foreign-flagged freighter awaits its turn at the grain elevator, and the small sturdy shrimp boats of the Mosquito Fleet return from the sea with thousands of screaming, chattering seabirds hovering over their wake. Reaching for the sky, the ANICO Building, our only skyscraper, stands like a marble sentinel watching over our town through a misty veil of fog.

Down 21st Street, the 1894 Grand Opera House is alive with music again, still embracing the ghosts of Bernhardt, Booth, and the legendary Lillie Langtry.

The Strand: "The More Things Change . . ."

More than one hundred years ago, Galveston's Strand, named after London's famed mercantile street, was the greatest banking and finance center between New Orleans and San Francisco. Today's mighty metropolis of Houston was a marshy, disease-ridden village of little consequence; proud Islanders called it Mudville—when, on very rare occasions, they had to refer to their northern neighbors.

"The story went," chronicles Gary Cartwright, "that an Islander attempting to cross one of Houston's boggy streets observed a sign that read 'NO BOTTOM!' True, there had been a time when pedestrians attempting to negotiate the Strand sank ankle-deep in sand, but by the 1890s, the Strand had elevated sidewalks, and was paved by wooden blocks—an impressive civic improvement, except during times of high tides when the Strand's pavement had an annoying tendency to float away."

Galveston's main business street, the Strand became known as the "Wall Street of the Southwest," and its ornate Victorian buildings were the envy of cities all over the country. Five of the largest banks in Texas were located on the Strand, as were eight newspapers. The block between 23rd and 24th streets was known as Insurance Square. Overall, by 1894 the city had six public squares, two parks, two miles of esplanade, street railways drawn by horses, thirteen hotels, three concert halls, and an opera house. Fancy shops sold fine English carpets, French china, wine and brandy, and German-made rosewood pianos. In 1858 alone, Islanders purchased twenty-three grand pianos. Galveston had the first gaslight, the first electric light, the first telephone, the first hospital, the first law firm, the first trade union, the first golf course . . . name any business or institution or invention, and Galveston probably had the first in Texas.

Cartwright captures the spirit of the Strand:

> The Strand was without question one of the most interesting streets anywhere. Restaurants like Monsieur Alphonse's specialized in dishes with names like "beefsteak goddam a la mode," and saloons like the Gem and the Age never closed. Sam's Club and Sample Room was a rendezvous for "mercantile gentlemen" and provided exchange newspapers, free meeting rooms, lunch and whiskey.
>
> The street stirred with activity and pulsed with strange sights. A long-haired, wild-eyed drummer who called himself the King of Pain sold patent medicine from his wagon, and strolling show people with trained monkeys and bears performed for coins on street corners. Some of the street characters were nearly mythical. An old pirate called Crazy Ben, who wore an earring and claimed to have been one of Lafitte's corsairs, paid for drinks with gold doubloons. Another man ate glass for tips, and was reported to have consumed a half-dozen lamp chimneys in a single afternoon. There were Mardi Gras parades, some of them costing ten thousand dollars or more, and circus parades; and on New Year's Day there was an annual extravaganza called the Parade of Butchers, in which butchers donned masks and marched in formation from saloon to saloon.

And that is the way it was a hundred years ago on The Strand—unique shops, trendy restaurants, strange characters, and a constantly changing kaleidoscope of people and activity. One must wonder if habitués of the nineteenth-century Strand would immediately notice the difference, were they plunked down on the Strand we all know and love today.

As the French say, *"Plus ça change, plus c'est la même chose . . ."*

One hundred years ago, the Strand was Galveston's "Main Street." The business district, with its ornate Victorian Buildings, stirred with activity and pulsed with some interesting, though perhaps strange, sights.
—Courtesy the Rosenberg Library

Lore, Legend, and Downright Lies

Friends, Romans . . .
Galvestonians?

When most of us think of the history of Galveston, our minds travel back in time no farther than the Karankawa Indians and Cabeza de Vaca, the Spanish explorer who landed on this Island in 1528. But Galveston's history may date back farther than we ever realized. Thanks to the curiosity of Valentine Belfiglio, a professor of history and international relations in Denton, Texas, there is another theory.

Belfiglio writes in the *Dallas Morning News* that he was intrigued by the notion that ancient Greeks or Romans might have voyaged to the New World. An unlikely source, *The Book of Mormon,* contains passages describing "barges that traveled the great sea that divideth the lands and came upon the shores of the promised land"—in Mormon theology, America.

Researching ancient writings, Belfiglio learned that the Romans knew the earth is round and that they were familiar with the Canary Islands, far out in the Atlantic. From those islands, currents sweep southwesterly, eventually past the tip of Florida and into the Gulf of Mexico. With this start, he began haunting museums and libraries in a search for more evidence. He found reports of a mysterious shipwreck and buried bridge timbers in Galveston Bay, accounts of Roman coins being unearthed, and apparent linguistic and cultural similarities between the Romans and the Karankawa Indians. The evidence was enough to convince Belfiglio. "I believe they were here," he says.

Roman coins have been discovered in this area and are still highly prized by treasure seekers.
—Robert John Mihovil

A visit to the Rosenberg Library uncovered an 1886 issue of the *Galveston Daily News* that reported the discovery of a wrecked ship of unusual design, a construction unlike what was then known of ships trading in the Gulf as far back as the 1500s. The vessel was said to be constructed of the most massive and solid oak planks, fully six or seven inches in thickness, the pieces laid crosswise over each other. Belfiglio consulted with archaeologists, who agreed that Roman sailors could have made it to the Gulf Coast by design or accident. Roman vessels were fully capable of sailing across the Atlantic—or being blown across it.

Belfiglio's excitement heightened when he read a 1915 news account of timbers found buried fifteen feet below the bottom of Galveston Bay—perhaps remnants of a Roman bridge? Two

Roman coins were recovered—one from a sandbar on St. Joseph's Island, another from the bottom of an Indian burial mound near Round Rock—a fact that would appear to date the Romans' arrival in the New World as sometime before 800 A.D.

Perhaps the most ingenious bit of research was a comparison of various words in Latin and the dialect of the Karankawa Indians, which seemed to turn up too many similarities to have been coincidental. Among the pairings were words for "house," "swim," "this," or "of that kind," and "jaws of death"—sharks, maybe? Also, the Karankawas, like the Romans, enjoyed wrestling, archery, and ball games.

Of course, there are those who disagree with the good doctor's theory. But whether our history dates back to Roman times or several centuries later, it's a fact that people have been warming their toes in the sun-baked sands of Galveston Island for a long, long time.

Jean Lafitte: The Heart of a Legend

The documented facts of Jean Lafitte are so fantastic, so dramatic, and so romantic that even Hollywood in its heyday may have hesitated to film the story—even with Errol Flynn swashing and buckling through the lead role. The force of Lafitte's character is such that the early history of Galveston *is* Lafitte. For Galveston, this aristocratic buccaneer wrote a flaming chapter of piracy, of heroism, of tender romance and of derring-do. He was a pirate, a patriot—and a lover.

The son of a French nobleman, Lafitte stowed away in his teens on a freighter, never to return to his homeland. At nineteen he married a dark-eyed beauty and outfitted a ship to carry cargo. A Spanish privateer took his money and his goods, scuttled his ship, put his crew in chains, and abandoned him and his young wife on a tiny island with few provisions. The couple was eventually rescued—but too late for Lafitte's wife. An American ship carried them to New Orleans, where she died.

Jim Nonus, third-generation B.O.I. (Born on the Island), is a member of the Jean Lafitte Society and impersonates the Island's famous pirate.
                                    —Courtesy Jim Nonus

Filled with sorrow, Lafitte vowed to avenge her death. He began a life of piracy and soon became wealthy and powerful. In 1813 Governor William Claiborne of Louisiana offered a $500 reward for Lafitte's capture. Lafitte, with a flair, retaliated with a reward of $15,000 for the capture of Claiborne.

In 1814, as Andrew Jackson and his men entered New Orleans to protect the Gulf Coast against British attack, an English delegation offered Lafitte $30,000 and a captaincy with full rank and honors if he would serve the Crown. Lafitte refused. Instead, he was granted immunity by Claiborne to fight the British. Lafitte and his pirates-turned-patriots are credited with much of the success of American arms in the Battle of New Orleans.

Lafitte was not meant for conventional life, however. Two years after the battle, in 1817, he moved to desolate, isolated Galveston Island, where he set up a miniature kingdom. Lafitte fitted out for himself an immense palace, half fort and half residence, on a site believed to be approximately where the Havre Lafitte subdivision stands today. From its color, the palace was known as the *Maison Rouge*, or "Red House." Finished and adorned with rich loot from captured vessels, it was indeed a home fit for a pirate king. Strangers were amazed at the grandeur of the place and the courtliness of the host. By this time, Jean had lost some of his youth, but none of his haughty, noble bearing.

In the year 1818 Lafitte stood at the height of his power. He dubbed himself "King of Campeche" (a name he gave his settlement on the Island), the "Lord of Galveston," and the "Terror of the Gulf." It was in that year that he met the great love of his life.

Madame Madeline Rigeaud was a tall blonde of striking appearance. In France, Madeline had been a professional nurse whose care had brought a wealthy aristocrat, General Rigeaud, back to health from an almost-fatal illness. In gratitude, the venerable old man offered Madeline his name and what was left of his fortune after the fall of the French Empire under Napoleon. In 1818 the general and Madeline sailed from France to join a colony of Frenchmen on the Trinity River in Texas.

When they reached Galveston, Lafitte entertained them with great courtesy at his famous Red House.

While reclining on a red velvet couch before a tawny leopard-skin rug, Lafitte took notice of Madame Rigeaud. Immediately, a spark was kindled. The next day, General and Madame Rigeaud left. Several months later the aged general died, and Madeline again passed through Galveston, heading back to France. She planned to buy a modest home and resume her nursing career.

Lafitte was aghast at the thought of this glorious creature

resigning herself to such an obscure fate. Such a waste! He offered marriage at once. Madeline, however, could not see herself as a pirate's wife, and she sailed at midnight on board the *Orléans* for France. The next day a violent hurricane hit Galveston. Lafitte, in a bold—many would say insane—venture, put his men aboard ship and sailed with the wind forcing his vessels across the Island itself and into the Gulf. The mad idea proved to be expedient, because soon his ships were in open water in comparative safety.

The next day Lafitte's men discovered the hull of a recently wrecked ship. It was the *Orléans*. Lafitte charged aboard, and with the superhuman strength of desperation, he made his way to the half-submerged cabin. He broke through the tumbled and splintered timbers and found Madeline lying unconscious in her bunk. Jean gathered her in his strong arms and took her to the Red House to recover. Luxuriously ensconced, Madeline had much time to think regarding her rescuer. Was he Lafitte the Pirate, Lafitte the Privateer, or Lafitte the Patriot? After hearing of his heroics in the Battle of New Orleans, and the praise from Andrew Jackson, Madeline became convinced that Lafitte was really a hero, an officer!

So Lafitte donned his captain's uniform and stood beside Madeline in the great hall of the Red House as they exchanged vows before an old French priest. Jean and Madeline lived together in happiness for many months. They expected an heir. This, however, was never to be. Madeline died in childbirth in late 1819 or 1820. Jean's world crumbled completely, and when the U.S. government decided to rid the coast of pirates, Lafitte put up little resistance. In 1820 he voluntarily destroyed the fort, set fire to the Red House with his own torch, and sailed away forever from Galveston Island.

In preparing to leave Galveston, Lafitte is said to have taken much of his fortune and buried it on the far western end of the Island, near "Three Trees," also known as "Lafitte's Cove." Despite their most diligent efforts, generations of treasure hunters have yet to uncover the cache.

Lafitte spent the remaining years of his life in Mexico's struggle for independence. He died and was buried on the Yucatán Peninsula.

These colorful pages in Galveston's history are recorded with the Jean Lafitte Society and are today acknowledged in the upscale West Isle development of Havre Lafitte, where Lafitte's lieutenants—Campbell, Lambert, Gerol, Lopez, Dominique You, Beluche, LeBrun, and Legas—are remembered in street names. Havre Lafitte's community house is named the Red House, and the community's beautiful lake is appropriately named after Madeline. Jean's brother, Pierre Lafitte, is also remembered. Havre Lafitte was developed to provide all the modern conveniences for good contemporary living, but always with a bow to the fascinating history of Galveston.

Bolivar Watermelon Man
Last of Lafitte's Corsairs

AN ESSAY BY JOEL KIRKPATRICK

[Editor's note: Among the colorful characters who peopled Galveston's waterfront in the heady years before the Great Storm was a grizzled old Bolivar farmer who sailed a scow schooner periodically to the bustling Isle docks to sell watermelons. To his customers and other dockside hangers-on, he would spin tales of a life at sea in the rollicking Age of Sail some seventy and eighty years earlier—particularly his service in the fleet of the legendary Jean Lafitte.

The record does not tell us how his tales were received, but we can imagine the snickers, the knowing smiles, the hints that the old man had been in the sun too long. After all, old men's "sea stories" more often than not were just that—stories. Sea stories or no, the Galveston Daily News saw fit to relate them, leaving us all to decide whether Charlie Cronea was just another old salt with a headful of yarns—or, indeed, the last of Jean Lafitte's storied buccaneer band. M.R.]

It has been more than one hundred years since Charlie Cronea sailed his butt-head schooner laden with watermelons to the docks in Galveston.

Cronea, a known member of the band of privateer Jean Lafitte, died March 4, 1893, at Rollover, near Gilchrist, at the age of eighty-eight. He lies buried in a small community ceme-

Charlie Cronea delivered his watermelons in a butt-head schooner like
these that were tied up at a dock in 1906.

—Courtesy Texas Maritime Museum

tery at High Island. The headstone of his grave, made of
beachshell concrete, has toppled, but a Texas State Historical
Association marker was erected at the site in 1997.

A year before his death, he came to Galveston aboard his produce schooner and was interviewed on the waterfront by one
Ben C. Smart, a reporter for *The Galveston Daily News*.

The reporter wrote, in a story found in the Rosenberg Library
archives, that Cronea told him he was a cabin boy in the crew of
Capt. James Campbell, whom Lafitte considered his most trusted
lieutenant. Cronea sailed with the crew on a topsail schooner in
the Gulf of Mexico for eight months, raiding Spanish shipping.

He told the reporter he had also fought in the Texas
Revolution with volunteers at San Jacinto and in the Mexican
War. In his later days, he no doubt told some tales that grew in

the telling. But those in the 1892 *Daily News* interview were included in Cronea's obituary, printed in the paper's March 6, 1893, edition.

"The death of Charles Cronea removes from Texas a peculiar man of whom little has been written, but whose history is as romantic as any man of the 19th Century," noted the *News*.

In the paper's 1892 story, the reporter said he had listened to Cronea, sitting in the barge office in Galveston, and heard the man reeling off yarn in "a mellow voice, taking pains to punctuate his assertions with the choicest profanity imaginable." He described Cronea as undersized, bright-eyed, and well preserved, with thin, silver hair and chin whiskers "as white as hair ever becomes."

Cronea, the newspaper story relates, told the reporter he was with Captain Campbell as a cabin boy. But he told others he was the cabin boy of Lafitte himself.

As Cronea told the *News* reporter:

> I was born in Marseilles, France on Jan. 14, 1805. In 1818 I shipped as a cabin boy aboard a French frigate bound for America, I was full of mischief and one day I cut up some trick that got me a round dozen on the bare back, My captain had me spread-eagled on a grating and had the boatswain give me a good dozen lashes with the cat.
>
> How it stung! And then they soused my back with seawater and it stung worse. But I never squealed. I made up my mind to run away when I got a chance.
>
> The frigate ran into New York harbor where I deserted her. This was in 1819. As soon as I could, I shipped on a vessel and went to Charleston, S.C. There I shipped in a bark bound for Liverpool.
>
> When we sailed out of Charleston harbor we hadn't cleared the bar by two hours when we hove to and a schooner which was running down on us luffed and sent a boat across.
>
> After a few minutes, the captain mustered all hands and we fell in to larboard.

Cronea told how the captain of the schooner wanted fifteen or twenty men to go on a cruise in the Gulf of Mexico.

> Well, 14 men besides myself agreed to sign on for the cruise and so we went aboard the schooner, commanded by a man from Baltimore named Jones.

Capt. Jones sailed away and we ran south along the coast, around the Keys and into the Gulf.

We kept out of the way of everything and flew American colors. We arrived off the beach near Corpus Christi and about 40 of us were set ashore. We had blankets and grub enough and our dunnage, so we didn't care much about being set ashore.

The next day, the schooner was gone, but in the afternoon, a hermaphrodite brig [schooner-brigantine] hove to off the beach and sent a boat ashore. The officer in charge told us we were to sail the brig, which he said was a privateer.

We all agreed to go, so we went aboard. The brig was under command of a man we knew as Carroll, but I afterward knew him as Capt. James Campbell. He was Lafitte's right-hand man.

You hear Lafitte was only a privateer, but I call him a pirut [sic]. That's what he was—a pirut.

The brig had a crew of about 80 men. She had a long Tom aft, two carronades on each side, and a bow-chaser on the forecastle.

The flag we hoisted was the Carthagenian [Republic of Cartagena] colors.

We cruised up and down the Gulf, capturing nothing but Spanish craft. If we saw one we did not know the nationality of, we signalled her to heave to.

If she didn't, we fired a round shot across her bow. That generally brought 'em to, and then the captain would call away a boat and send a crew and an officer, all armed, aboard.

If the vessel was Spanish, we could break out as much of the cargo as we needed, taking particular pains to get tobacco. Then we would take her crew aboard the brig and scuttle the Spanish ship, setting it on fire. The crew we would set ashore along the coast.

Sometimes a Spaniard would show fight and our gunner would send a round shot into her. Then you would hear the Spanish yell and holler at us. They always surrendered quickly after that. A good many think we used to cut throats and make some captives walk the plank. But that is all a lie. I never saw a man murdered while I was with Campbell.

Cronea told of spilling a bucket of water on Campbell's feet and being forced to stand on the breech of a pivot gun for half an hour. He said he made up his mind to run away, and did so when the brig put into Mermanteau, Louisiana, in late 1820.

"I came to Galveston Island in 1821. There was but one or two shanties here then and Lafitte had gone away," he told the reporter.

He said he was a member of Capt. David Garner's company, mustered in Orange County, and was in the siege of San Antonio de Bexar before the battle of the Alamo. Although he protested that he never was awarded any land as a surviving soldier of the Texas Revolution, records show that he was awarded veteran's donation No. 1153 for 1,280 acres of land on January 24, 1885.

Cronea moved to High Island around 1875 from near Old Jefferson, Texas (near present-day Bridge City).

Although Cronea is reported to have told his son-in-law, Henry Sullivan of High Island, stories of pirates, the sea, the revolution, and buried treasure, none of the stories he told during his lifetime except the one in the *News* are known to have survived.

What is worth noting is that the historical events for which Charles Cronea is remembered constituted only a fraction of his life. He lived nearly all that life as a farmer in this part of Texas, raised children as well as crops, and saw much more saltwater from the tiller of a watermelon-laden "butt-head" schooner than from the gun deck of a pirate ship.

Cronea and the son-in-law who married his daughter Louise are buried in the cemetery near the Gulf of Mexico on the seaward crest of High Island Hill. Some of Cronea's descendants are buried around him, people with names like Breaux, Dailey, and Sullivan.

"Think Snow—But Carefully!"

Not long ago, longtime friends from Canada came for a holiday, and as we talked about Galveston and its history they wondered if it ever snowed this far south. Well, as far back as Maury Darst, the late, great reporter of Galveston history, could trace the weather reports, he found two major snowstorms that swept across the Island in the late 1800s. So there have been times (not in the summer, though!) when snow has blanketed Galveston, and Galveston Bay actually froze over.

The first big snow swept through on January 12, 1886, and the second on February 14, 1895. Islanders fashioned sleds, and neighbors engaged in snowball fights. Galveston was transformed into a winter wonderland on that 1895 Valentine's Day, with snowdrifts banked in streets from Galveston to League City. Icicles hung from buildings, tree limbs, and the spars and rigging of the sailing ships in Galveston Harbor. Business was suspended throughout the county, and in Galveston streetcars ceased operations. Wagons that tried to crawl through the snow found themselves mired in drifts.

One of the few Islanders to venture out into the frozen wonderland was the late Marsene Johnson, Sr., who at the time held the position of city recorder. Needless to say, he had few followers. Johnson also called W. S. Sinclair, operator of the Beach Hotel, and offered to send out a plow to rescue the hotel from its burial under a mass of snow and ice.

Trains of the Galveston, Houston and Henderson Railroad failed to leave Houston due to the heavy snowfall in the Bayou City, and most of the tracks were buried under the white blanket. Along the waterfront, many ships were frozen at their docks and hundreds of cotton bales were covered with up to fifteen inches of the white powder. Weather Bureau recorders show a total snowfall of 15.2 inches and temperatures at a steady 24 degrees and lower over a period of several days, accompanied by heavy wind gusts.

Hack drivers did a land-office business taking sightseers on tours for $20 a ride. Alderman Joe Levy was seen gliding over the snow in a wagon mounted on runners, and Joseph Seinsheimer mounted his buggy on runners to see the sights.

One Galvestonian, Hart Settle, attached his horse to a skiff and had a fine time sleighing "à la Laplander" with his family.

No one took a dip in the Gulf of Mexico, although it was one of the few bodies of water in the entire country that did not freeze over. More recently, we have experienced two back-to-back "White Christmases," in 1989 and 1990. They were just the lightest dustings, but the snowfalls nevertheless enchanted both the young and young at heart with the perfect fairyland setting for Santa to arrive with his sleigh full of toys pulled by eight tiny reindeer.

Yes, that's one way to feel cooler on a sticky summer's day: Just "think snow," and recall a cool memory of the times Mother Nature covered even this tropic isle with a white, wintry blanket.

The Beach Hotel was transformed into a winter wonderland on Valentine's Day 1895 when the Weather Bureau recorders showed a snowfall of 15.2 inches.

—Courtesy the Rosenberg Library

Galveston's "Golden Age":
Burning the Candle at Both Ends

Back in the middle twenties, skirts were short, women bobbed their hair, the dance craze was the Charleston, and Rudy Vallee crooned his "Maine Stein Song" to the young ladies known as flappers.

And here on Galveston Island, the first big-time night club opened its doors. Harold Scarlett described the club in the *Houston Chronicle*:

> The Hollywood Dinner Club was built from the ground up at 61st Street and Avenue S, on the western edge of the city, beyond the end of the Seawall. Instantly, it was the swankiest night spot on the Gulf Coast—Spanish architecture, crystal chandeliers, rattan furniture, a dance floor bigger than the ballroom at the Galvez Hotel. And air conditioning! The Hollywood was the very first air-conditioned night club in the country. Sam Maceo gave instructions that the temperature be maintained at 69 degrees on the theory that drinkers who were cool didn't feel the booze, and drinkers who didn't feel the booze were lousy performers at the crap tables . . .

> But Sam Maceo was the consumate showman. He made certain that the high rollers all over Texas heard about the Hollywood Dinner Club. A pair of searchlights out front made the place impossible to miss. For opening night Sam booked Guy Lombardo and his Royal Canadians, one of the biggest names in the business. The club drew 20,000 customers during Lombardo's three-week engagement. In the months that followed, Sam brought in only the biggest names—Ray Noble's band with Glenn Miller playing first trombone, Sophie Tucker, Joe E. Lewis, the Ritz Brothers.

> Rhumba contests, offering first prizes of $1,000, lured some of the best dancers in the country. A young hoofer named Fred Astaire was the Hollywood Dinner Club's resident dance instructor for a while. The country's first remote radio broadcast originated at the Hollywood, featuring Ben Bernie and All the Boys.

> And where but in Galveston could Bernie ad-lib to the folks out in radioland, "Am I welcome here? Even the water is coming

in to greet me!" as the club sat surrounded by two feet of saltwa-ter—pushed inland by a hurricane.

Stations all over the Midwest picked it up. Phil Harris and a number of other stars got national attention by way of the radio hookup. A young musician from Beaumont sat in one night when the regular trumpet player was drunk and he got regular work with the band. His name was Harry James.

The opening of the Hollywood was a landmark event, not just in Texas but nationwide. Nobody had ever offered the public gambling, gourmet food, and top-name entertainment all under one roof. (Remember, this was 1926, years before there was a Strip in Las Vegas.)

The Grotto, another well-known dining club with gambling, opened shortly after the Hollywood. This club was located at Seawall Boulevard and 21st Street. Standing out over the water on piers, it was damaged by a storm, and when it reopened it was called the Sui Jen. It served a Chinese menu and was admired for its pagoda-shaped bandstand.

And then there was the Balinese Room.

Ah, what memories! The Balinese was considered the flagship of the Island casinos. It offered an exotic South Seas decor, impeccable service, elegant food—and in the back room, a strictly illegal, but highly patronized, dice and roulette casino.

One night in the 1940s, recalls former *Houston Post* writer Harold Scarlett, a Houston businessman was rolling the dice in the Balinese Room, and he was hot—but his wife was tired and fidgety. It was getting on toward sunrise, and she kept nagging her husband to take her home.

"Aw, go jump overboard," he told her offhandedly, brandish-ing the dice for another toss. His wife rose casually and strolled out onto the open balcony. The wind whipped her dress as she dived into the churning surf thirty feet below.

Ignoring the shouts of alarm, her husband kept caressing the dice. A distraught dealer raced to her rescue. In his excitement, he tried to dive through a thick-paned window. He was taken to a hospital with head cuts and a concussion. The spurned wife swam to shore, strolled dripping wet back into the casino, and calmly finished her drink.

"Have a nice swim, honey?" her husband asked. He had never stopped rolling the dice. That was the Balinese Room in its heyday.

The Studio Lounge was on the second floor of the Turf Athletic Club in a three-story building on 23rd between Market and Postoffice. Gary Cartwright describes the lounge: "The second floor was secured by a private elevator and an electronic buzzer system that was highly sophisticated for its time. The floor was divided into two sections: a bar and nightclub called the Studio Lounge, decorated in Art Deco fashion, with murals, black lights, and mirrors trimmed in zebra skin; and a second bar and restaurant called the Western Room."

These establishments brought prominence and notoriety and an enduring nickname to the Island. For the next three decades, it was known as the "Free State of Galveston."

The music stopped in 1957, when Texas Attorney General Will Wilson made good on his promise to shut down gambling in Galveston County. All the slot machines wound up at the bottom

The Balinese was considered the flagship of the Island casinos. The long walkway to the gambling rooms provided the time necessary to hide the gaming tables from the prying eyes of the law when they entered to seek evidence of illegal gambling.

—Robert John Mihovil

of Galveston Bay—such a big pile, in fact, that it is said the site was once marked on nautical charts as a hazard to navigation. One by one, the Turf Club, the Studio Lounge, and the other glittering pleasure palaces disappeared. There's a self-serve filling station where the Hollywood Dinner Club once stood; only the derelict shell of the Balinese Room, tottering on sea-worn pilings over the Gulf at 21st Street, remains as a silent witness to a time many Islanders still call Galveston's "Golden Age."

Undeniably, the clubs and casinos brought glamour to Galveston along with the gambling. Although there are those who long for the wide-open days, others look back on the time as a bad dream that blighted the Island's progress and growth. Either way, there are precious few who believe those days will ever return.

As Harold Scarlett observed, "Galveston, to paraphrase the poet, burned its candle at both ends, and it didn't last the night.

"But oh, it made a lusty light!"

From "Love by the Ton" to Mortified Church Ladies, Postoffice Street Has Seen It All

"A hick town is a town with no place to go that you shouldn't." So said Sam Maceo, Galveston's "Godfather," in 1950. Well, we all know that Galveston has never qualified as a hick town. Right?

Geography gave Galveston some natural advantages. Smugglers had plied their trade through the surrounding coves and inlets since the beginning—pirates, privateers, and pioneers alike.

Galveston was notorious for bootlegging in the 1920s and 30s and wide-open gambling in the 40s and 50s. But Galveston did not discover these activities; they had been prevalent all over Texas from the earliest days. Galveston just continued to drink and gamble long after the rest of Texas had ceased these pastimes—or gone underground with them.

The Texas Heroes Monument officially points her finger to the San Jacinto monument . . . but unofficially it is said that her outstretched arm points the way to the pleasure palaces on Postoffice Street.
—Courtesy Robert John Mihovil

But what you may not realize is that Galveston's reputation for shady activities probably started on Postoffice Street around the end of the nineteenth century.

A number of respectable families had lived there before, but the houses along Postffice between 25th and 30th streets were being converted into bawdy houses by the 1890s. The red-light district grew until it spilled over into the side streets and onto part of Church Street, and the district flourished for more than sixty years.

Best estimates are that at the district's height there must have been twenty of these pleasure palaces, each headed by a madam, or "landlady," and each with six to ten girls working on a regular basis. Each house had servants and was equipped with a bar in the parlor, and most had some kind of music. Some had player pianos operated with nickels for dancing; others had jukeboxes, and some even provided live music.

The landlady lived downstairs or in back and the girls lived upstairs. Some of the houses displayed red lights; others maintained elegant facades and were luxuriously furnished. A few houses featured scantily clad girls sitting in the windows, while other girls wore long evening dresses.

Bouncers hired for protection kept down the kind of incidents that might attract the police. The district had a reputation as a fairly safe place during its heyday. There were stories about kind-hearted madams safeguarding the valuables of customers who might have had too much to drink. There were stories about customers getting rolled and then recovering their money with the help of the district's own security force.

Harold Scarlett tells a classic tale of the red-light district:

> The madams of Postoffice served seamen, soldiers, and socialites with gowned courtesans of every skin hue and shape. One place specialized in fat *femmes fatales* and advertised "Love by the Ton."
>
> As for themselves, the madams of those bygone days were sometimes regal and cultured creatures. Perhaps the last of these was Queen Laura, with her cascade of ebony hair so long it brushed the floor. She was still around in the early days of Prohibition.
>
> Madams had a certain flair. One was famous for the magnificent Christmas decorations with which she adorned her home (not her place of business). Every Yuletide, crowds congregated in the street to "ooh" and "aah."
>
> An earlier era, however, produced what is probably the all-time prize story about Galveston's red-light district.
>
> It concerned a group of church ladies who visited the house of a madam named Cora in an effort to set the soiled doves on the path to salvation.
>
> As the church crusaders prayed in the parlor, a man breezed in with easy familiarity and warbled, "Hey Cora, where's my baby Helen?" One of the church ladies melted to the floor in a faint. The man was her husband.

Galveston just plain did not go along with the new morality when the rest of the state did—which was not, however, to say that being a Galvestonian automatically meant you were "connected."

Very few Galveston people were involved in bootlegging, but many Galvestonians bought bootlegged merchandise. Very few Galveston people were actually involved in gambling. Most of the patrons came from somewhere else. Employees were well paid. They paid their taxes and gave generously to churches and charities.

Galveston's attitude toward drinking, gambling, and prostitution was one of cheerful toleration. This attitude was contrary to the prevailing sentiment in Texas. But we have never been embarrassed about being different. Galveston lives as comfortably with its history as any city I know.

It has been said that the Texas Heroes Monument at Broadway and 25th Street, rising majestically above the traffic below, pointed with her outstretched arm the way for young student visitors seeking Galveston's pleasure palaces on Postoffice Street. Oh, what stories that statue could tell!

And sometimes . . . at dusk . . . when the fading sun slides low in the west . . . I understand if you listen carefully, you'll hear her whisper, "Just over there . . . just down the street," . . . on beautiful, historic Galveston Island.

Isolated Beaches Drew More Than Beachcombers During Prohibition Era

During the Prohibition era, this lovely little isle was discovered by Caribbean rumrunners. Gary Cartwright explains:

> Starting in the spring of 1919, schooners from Cuba, Jamaica, and the Bahamas began running liquor to the Island—up to 20,000 cases at a time. The ships dropped anchor 35 miles out at sea, at a rendezvous point southwest of Galveston called Rum Row, and the booze was offloaded into small powerboats or flat-bottomed launches for delivery to spots along the miles of deserted beach.

One enterprising Galvestonian, a member of the rumrunning "Beach Gang," would take his little granddaughter out for midnight walks on the beach on moonless nights, genially allowing her to carry the lantern to light their way. She was delighted with these late-night adventures—never knowing that as she skipped down the beach, swinging Grandpa's lantern, she was signaling "all clear" to the small boats waiting offshore to deliver their illicit cargo.

According to Cartwright, "The boats slipped in under the cover of darkness and

> beached in shallow water, where work crews waded out and carried the goods to shore. Each case was wrapped in a burlap sack, and two sacks were tied together for easy handling. Sometimes the goods were delivered to remote piers at Offatt's Bayou, or to one of the secluded coves near San Luis Pass. On rare occasions liquor was even unloaded at one of the out-of-the-way piers at the port, the same as coffee, bananas, and other legal delicacies. From there it was either stored in dock warehouses to await transportation, or immediately loaded into trucks and freighted off the island. Galveston became a main supplier of bootleg liquor for Dallas, Houston, Denver, St. Louis, Omaha, and other thirsty cities in the Southwest and Midwest. . . .
>
> Eventually two rival rum-running gangs divided up the Island, using Broadway as a line of demarcation. The Beach gang, so

called because it landed most of its goods on West Beach, occupied the south half of the Island . . . . The other major smuggling outfit, the Downtown Gang, was distinguished by its reputation for having considerably more brass than brains.

Out of these two gangs rose one of Galveston's most colorful characters, who led the Downtown Gang. Always wearing a diamond stickpin and carrying a wad of $100 bills at least two inches thick, he was a generous man who gave toys to children at Christmas, and it is rumored that he spent $40,000 on a party at New York's Pennsylvania Hotel, where stars of the silent screen Nancy Carroll and Clara Bow frolicked in a bath of costly champagne.

"He was equally famous for his careless approach to business. He sometimes hijacked truckloads of booze belonging to rival smugglers, and once stiffed a group of Cubans by paying for their boatload of rum with—of all things—soap coupons," continues Cartwright.

So brazen was this gang leader that he once had his crew unload a shipment on the jetty only 200 yards from the Coast Guard station. He owned the fastest boat on the Gulf, a gasoline launch, and one of his favorite sports was outrunning Coast Guard vessels.

As might be expected, the gangster's brash manner proved his downfall after he was finally grabbed by federal agents near Offatt's Bayou.

Standing before the judge, he was very self-assured. When the judge set his fine at $5,000, the brazen smuggler grinned and retorted, "Hell, Judge, I've got that much in my right-hand pocket." The judge, unimpressed, said, "Then look in your left-hand pocket and see if you can find two years in the federal pen at Leavenworth."

The repeal of Prohibition in 1933 ushered out the age of bathtub gin, speakeasies, and the brassy, brazen souls who ferried illicit booze onto Isle shores. But the gamblers and the "ladies of negotiable affections" plied their trades unhindered; indeed, it would be another quarter-century before the heavy hand of the law brought a final end to the "Golden Age" on Galveston Island.

Grandpa's lantern, carried by his grandaughter, would signal "all clear" to rumrunners so that they could launch small skiffs to carry their illegal liquid cargo ashore.

—Robert John Mihovil

World War II: Sailors, Sheep, and Swine Kept Pelican Island Safe for Democracy

How many of us today recall the days of World War II? Does it really seem like more than fifty years ago that we may have been listening to a shortwave radio, hearing the Führer's voice ranting, almost animal-like—or having our fears calmed by the firm, assuring words of Franklin D. Roosevelt? Perhaps we gained strength when we listened to the song lyrics, "There'll be bluebirds over / The white cliffs of Dover / Tomorrow, when the world is free."

And how many remember when the United States Navy maintained a "frontier base" on Pelican Island?

At the time, the Pelican Island Causeway did not exist, and the island was accessible only by government launches or a ferry operated by Todd Shipyards. Buses would pick up sailors quartered at the Galvez Hotel and take them to the dock. Even by ferry, it was still a long walk through thick underbrush to the navy reservation.

Early in the war, submarine chasers operated out of this frontier base, escorting ships out of port, ever vigilant for the Nazi submarines that lurked beneath the placid Gulf waters. Ashore, the first lieutenant in charge of base maintenance was responsible for the six boats that provided the only transportation to and from Galveston; and twenty-seven vehicles on Galveston Island and three on Pelican, including a truck, a bulldozer, and a jeep. He also was in charge of the pig herd, which ate the garbage, and the flock of sheep, which mowed the grass.

The base also housed a supply depot. Reinforced-concrete bunkers were used to store depth charges and ammunition for the sub chasers and tankers sailing from Texas City and other Galveston Bay petrochemical ports, which were armed with five-inch guns. The navy base also had two barracks buildings, a power plant, an administration building, and a galley. The galley never encountered any garbage-disposal problems—that's what the pigs were there for. Morning formation, or "quarters," was never held. The mosquitoes were in charge at that time of day and did not permit it.

Today, traces of this frontier navy base are hard to find, but if you look carefully on the eastern portion of Pelican Island, you may find sections of an old chain-link fence, a few rotting creosoted poles, complete with light fixtures, and several concrete ammunition bunkers, now stripped of their earth-and-grass covering.

This navy installation was a rather well-kept secret. Not many Galvestonians knew about it, although the young men who were stationed there will no doubt never forget those days—slopping the hogs, swatting mosquitoes, and otherwise keeping the world safe for democracy, just a ferry ride away from historic, romantic, beautiful Galveston Island.

Navy vessels wait at Todd Shipyards off Pelican Island for a call to escort merchant ships through the dangerous Gulf waters, always on the watch for enemy submarines.

—Courtesy Galveston Maritime Union

Semper Fi: Isle Marines March Off to War—and Rivalry

On Galveston Island, we dedicate July 4th to the armed forces of the United States of America. Today, we pay a tribute to the United States Marines—in particular the marines from Galveston. In August of 1936 the first Galveston Marine Corps Reserve unit was activated, with Lt. Col. Clark W. Thompson assigned as the unit's first commanding officer. Married to Libbie Moody, daughter of Isle financial mogul W. L. Moody, Jr., Thompson was the catalyst and founder of the Marine Reserve in Galveston.

In the fall of 1940, this unit was designated as the Fifteenth Infantry Battalion and was among the first reserve units called to active duty during World War II. Leaving the Island for San Diego, California, they were divided and went their separate ways—some went to Iceland, while others were among the first combat forces to leave the United States after Pearl Harbor. Some went to Samoa, and some landed on Guadalcanal, becoming what we might call "lean and mean Marines": lean because there was not much to eat there, and mean . . . well, maybe because they didn't receive their pay for the sixteen months they were there.

When the marines moved from the battle-scarred South Pacific islands to Wellington, New Zealand, the citizens welcomed them with a huge celebration. Later, the marines who had been serving in Iceland sent word that they were coming to help finish the job in the Pacific—and, as you can imagine, the rivalry escalated.

The Iceland troops arrived dressed in crisp green uniforms—and all wearing the Fourragère, or "Thicket," an award from the French government commemorating the unit's service a quarter-century earlier during World War I's Battle of Belleau Wood. The award was not a medal, but rather a golden rope looped over the shoulder. The marines who had been fighting in the Pacific bristled at the suggestion that they needed any help from Iceland and spread the word that any marine with a gold rope wore it to warn others that he carried a contagious disease! Needless to say, the good citizens of New Zealand threw no celebrations upon their arrival.

Colonel Lee Weber of
the Fifteenth Infantry
Battalion . . . from
Galveston to Guad-
alcanal and back.
—Courtesy Lee Weber

The sixteen months' back pay owed to the Pacific Marines finally caught up with them in Wellington. Immediately, they became very wealthy in relation to the other servicemen in New Zealand. With money in their pockets, the United States Marines wined and dined all the pretty girls in Wellington.

But somehow, I think that these marines would have won the hearts of these young ladies even without the extra pay—just as they have won the many wars they fought.

The City of Galveston Flies Off to War

In 1940 ominous rumors rumbled throughout the world of Hitler's war spreading from Europe to the Pacific and plunging the United States into a worldwide conflict. Galveston feared that, as an important oil tanker port, it might be an enemy target. Isle Mayor Brently Harris called for meetings with city and county officials to make contingency plans and to decide how and when to take action. The Red Cross was activated, the call went out for civil-defense volunteers, and the coastal cities installed warning sirens.

All this preparedness did not escape the notice of young John Miranda. John had come to Galveston with his family when he was just a year old. After graduating from Ball High, he went to Texas A&M University, where he decided he had better prepare himself for the war that he knew was about to engulf this country. So, as many young men did, John went to Canada to join the Canadian Air Force.

As soon as he was awarded his wings, he returned to Galveston to claim his bride. John and Paula Sharp had met at a friend's home, and after their marriage they returned together to Canada. But not for long—the events in Hawaii at Pearl Harbor had changed everything. The United States sent a train to Canada with army, navy, marine and air force recruiters to sign up young men for the United States armed forces. Of course, John signed up for the United States Army Air Corps.

Sent to Salina, Kansas, he became captain of a B-29. A crew was assembled, and they trained together. On overseas training flights, Galveston was their designated port of entry, so each time they came through they spent the night. Their first stop was always the buffet at Southern Select, followed by an evening of entertainment at the Balinese Room. The Maceos, who operated the Balinese as well as most of the Island's other dining, dancing, and gambling spots, appreciated the men who were serving their country and wanted them to have a good time in their establishment—and as luck would have it, John and his crew always won enough to pay for their parties in Galveston.

Who is to say whether it was luck—or a salute from the house?

At any rate, the overseas assignment for John's B-29 and its crew was Guam. The ship needed a name, of course, so the crew members (there were twelve of them) each wrote a name on a slip of paper, put the slips in a hat, and drew one. The winner was "The City of Galveston." John was pleased, and even more so when he discovered all of the slips in the hat bore the name "City of Galveston." The plane also had a second name that expressed the feelings of the captain and crew: "Peacemaker."

Bombing runs over Japan were long and tiring and for the most part fairly routine, until the fateful day when, passing over Nagoya, heading for the open Pacific and home base, the *City of Galveston* was hit by enemy fire. The wings were damaged, the bomb bay door was blasted off, and the radio was no longer operating. As the crippled plane limped out over the open water, a submarine was spotted. Captain Miranda guided the aircraft over the vessel and all bailed out. The parachuting airmen landed safely in the water, scattered along a mile-long path. In only about an hour and a half, the submarine had them all aboard and accounted for.

This B-29, based on Tinian Island in the South Pacific during World War II, like the City of Galveston, *finished the war against Japan.*
—Donald B. Fendler, 20th Air Force, 482nd squadron, 505th bomb group.

For seven days, the crew of the *City of Galveston* were guests of the navy. They had no chance to celebrate their rescue; they were always subject to depth-charge attacks, as they were in enemy territory. The hard part for these flyboys was the absolute silence they lived in for that week. Finally, a second submarine arrived, both vessels surfaced, and rubber rafts transferred the airmen to a submarine headed for Guam.

After a ten-day rest in Hawaii, it was back to work. A new B-29 was ready, again named "City of Galveston"—and on the other side was the name "Pentado," the submarine that had saved their lives. No longer under a rule of silence, the celebration of life and the christening of the new *City of Galveston* were combined. This time, the crew of the submarine *Pentado* were the guests of the airmen. John Miranda was awarded the Silver Star for the safe return of his crew and later was promoted to colonel.

Texas Tradition Takes a Twist with Bolivar Goat Roundup

You never hear the old familiar song "I'm Headin' for the Last Roundup" without thinking of Texas. Even in this Gulf Coastal area, cattle raising, rodeos, and calf roping were a part of life. Ranching ruled Bolivar Peninsula from the very beginning. In the early '20s, when pasture land grew scarce, some of the men took their horses to Orange for grazing. When they returned to get them several months later, the landowner told them their horses had "died," or "gotten lost," and he gave them an equal number of goats instead.

So, goat raising took the place of cattle raising on the peninsula, and the rodeos continued—with the cowboys roping the billies instead of the calves. After the dredging of the Intracoastal Waterway isolated the goats on a spoil island across from Bolivar proper, the cowboys (or should I say goatboys?) initiated a goat roundup every year in late June. There was a reason for this—culling a few and holding a big goat barbecue was a great way to prepare a feast for the July 4th picnics.

Wonder how the roundup participants got across the busy Intracoastal to the appropriately named Goat Island with their horses? It was quite an operation: The riders put their saddles in motorboats, tied the horses behind the boats, and swam them across. A true father-and-son operation, the younger boys led the horses into the water while the dads ran the boats.

And once they were landed on the island and saddled up, the fun had just begun, for they next had to find the goats, which were scattered all over the scrubby little islet, half hidden in the weeds and bushes. They herded them into a small arena, and the boys and their fathers ran around roping the scampering billies. The "lucky" goats were loaded onto a barge and taken back to Port Bolivar.

The last goat roundups were organized by Pike Kahla and Joe Bill Kahla, who were owners of the last two herds. In *They Made Their Own Law,* Melanie Wiggins writes,

> In spite of all the hardships, "Uncle Pike," as everyone calls him, carries on his roundups. Each year could be the last. The 84-yr-old cattleman has a hard time recruiting enough experienced cowboys, and some of those are afraid to swim their expensive horses across the ever-widening canal. . . . So the problems get tougher, but Uncle Pike goes on, undaunted. In his battered straw hat and overalls, he stands firm at his command post in a field of swirling goats or steers, shouting curses and waving his cane at the cowboys, who are his sons, grandsons and nephews.
>
> In the summer of 1989 this patriarch of the peninsula insisted on staging the goat roundup even though a raging storm had set in, and the bedraggled participants, clad in plastic garbage sacks, rounded up a few wet goats. . . . A TV man from Houston had promised to come out and film the whole event but failed to show up because of the weather. Uncle Pike, sorely disappointed, said, "We'll just have to do the gol-darned thing again next year!"

Unfortunately, the last word from the Peninsula was that the annual goat roundups had ceased—thanks, apparently, in no small part to towboat operators on the Intracoastal who discovered this fortuitous supply of free-range cabrito and took to

tying up alongside Goat Island at sundown and helping themselves to barbecued goat on the decks of their vessels.

Galveston Island and its neighbor, Bolivar Peninsula—one
embraced entirely by water, the other anchored to the continent.
Both share a colorful history and a host of legends, memories,
and ghosts who leave their indelible footprints in the sands of
our Gulf-washed shores.

*Two young cowboys (goatboys) wrestle with a stubborn animal at the
Bolivar goat roundup.*

— Melanie Wiggins

Galveston's Ghosts: How Many "D.O.I.s" Haunt Isle Nights?

Here on our lovely island on sultry summer days, the wind blows straight out of the tropics—sometimes wet, sometimes mean, and always hot. We're still ten degrees cooler than Houston, though, due perhaps—at least in part—to the chilling stories of Galveston's ghosts.

Noted author Gary Cartwright once wrote:

> I never go back to the Island without sensing the ghosts. I can't think of a place where they run thicker. . . . Coming down the coastal prairie from Houston on Interstate 45 you can smell the ghosts before you see or hear them. They smell sweet and moldy, like the unfocused memory of some lost sensation jarred unexpectedly to mind. It's the scent of tangled gardens of jasmine, honeysuckle and magnolia, maybe. Or the smell of decaying timbers of shipwrecks, half-buried in the sand, or the weathered salt-caked planking of abandoned cotton warehouses stretching between the highway and the wharves. Encoded in the smells are secrets so fleeting that just thinking about them causes them to vanish. . . . The causeway empties onto Broadway and the ghosts take form and begin to murmur.

Ashton Villa, home of the Brown family, is a lovely Victorian mansion on Broadway. Daughter Miss Bettie Brown "scandalized Islanders in the 1880s by smoking cigarettes in public and racing unchaperoned along Broadway in a carriage pulled by teams of matched stallions—a black pair for day and a white pair for evening. It is said that on occasion Miss Brown's ghost appears in the dead of night and plays the piano in the villa's 'Gold Room,'" Cartwright informs us. And more recently, at a Christmas party held in the ballroom of Ashton Villa, four guests named Brown each had their names drawn for door prizes. Miss Bettie was taking care of the Browns. How do I know this? I was one of those Browns.

Remember the Old Galveston Club, hidden away in the back of the Interurban Queen newsstand at Market and 21st Street?

The sign on the building read, "The Last of the Old Speakeasys."

Cartwright describes the club:

> You could almost smell the beer on the ghosts. The bartender, Santos Cruz, claims to have invented the Margarita in honor of Peggy Lee when he was mixing drinks in the Balinese Room in 1948. The Club is dark and smells faintly rancid, like pulverized popcorn ground into the floor of old movie houses. From the glow of beer signs you could see oil portraits of nude beauties hanging on the south wall.

All seven of them were local models, and most of them are grandmothers today.

The Old Galveston Club is gone, torn down for a parking lot in a middle-of-the-night demolition not long ago. But Santos is not a ghost. He still tends bar, now in his own club. And the beauties whose portraits graced the south wall of the club aren't ghosts, either. But the ghosts, they say, still haunt the alley that runs behind the Opera House, where the Old Galveston Club once stood, looking for a cool brew on a warm summer's night.

On the Strand is a group of buildings called Hendley Row, the oldest commercial block on the Island. Built in 1858, the four-story structure was a lookout post during the Civil War for both Union and Confederate troops. You can still see marks of cannonballs on the 20th Street side. Today, says Cartwright, the upstairs are apartments where tenants, mostly a "fun-loving group of would-be actors, writers and artists, live happily with the ghosts of the Sacred Order of the JOLO (no one seems to know what the letters signify) who stood watch on the roof of the Hendley Building during the War."

Down on the West End, a few years ago, before subdivisions expanded, you could go look for the spot where Cabeza de Vaca and his wretched crew crawled ashore after they were shipwrecked in 1588. Just at sunrise, go down to the water . . . walk along the narrow beach and at the rack line find shells and driftwood washed up by the tide. Stand on the dunes with your back to the surf and imagine what Cabeza must have seen. Countless storms and flood tides have changed the face of the beach, but still standing is a small grove of trees. As a soft breeze touches

At the end of Galveston's airport was the old Magnolia Grove Cemetery. Pictured are graves in the Masonic Court of Honor.
—Courtesy the Rosenberg Library

the back of your neck, you may barely hear a voice whispering. "If you were shipwrecked," it asks, "what would you do?"

"But of course, I'd head straight for that grove of trees," you answer. Many believe Cabeza de Vaca and his crew did just that.

As pilots line up their final approach for landing at Scholes Field, many are unaware that Galveston ghosts are dancing at the end of the runway. You see, underneath the runway is a graveyard. Jim Brigance explains:

> Magnolia Cemetery was established in 1870. But somehow, after the hurricane of 1875 and the big one in 1900, the association that maintained the cemetery went bankrupt. However, that didn't keep people from dying and it didn't stop people from burying folks in the Magnolia Cemetery.

As time passed, though, many land transactions ensued, and the cemetery restrictions strangely disappeared. By the early 1930s, a small city airport had cropped up just east of the old and almost-forgotten Magnolia Cemetery. In 1939 the army decided Fort Crockett's little airfield wasn't big enough to cope with a war they feared was coming. Remember, by 1941 America had sold Japan enough scrap iron and steel to start worrying whether we might get it back—in the form of bombs and bullets—and so the old Magnolia Cemetery land was paved over as a runway for the heavy bombers based at Scholes Field.

It's a little hard to imagine building an airfield on top of a graveyard today without drawing a flurry of lawsuits. But at the time, we had to stop three stooges named Hitler, Tojo, and Mussolini.

We truly love our Galveston ghosts . . . those who play the piano in the darkest hours . . . who search for a cool brew in the shadows of a dim alley . . . the shipwrecked sailors on a not-so-deserted island . . . and, of course, the light-footed wraiths dancing on moonbeams at the end of the Scholes Field runway.

Demolition Banishes More Than Just Old Buildings

AN ESSAY BY MAX RIZLEY, JR.

They blew up the old Buccaneer Hotel in Galveston on New Year's Day, 1999.

Or, more properly, they blew *down* the Buccaneer, using a series of deftly placed and timed dynamite blasts to collapse the seventy-year-old Seawall landmark into itself, leaving a neat pile of rubble (if a pile of rubble can be called "neat") sitting precisely on the block where seconds earlier had stood an eleven-story building.

It had to come down, we are told; the old hotel building was structurally unsound, and the cost of rehabilitating it versus the

You always hate to see a venerable landmark like the Buccaneer Hotel go down as it did on January 1, 1999. Though the building is gone, the memories will always remain.

—Robert John Mihovil

potential market for big, old hotel buildings just didn't balance out.

Still, you always hate to see a venerable landmark like the Buccaneer go. The simple loss of its sheer bulk alters the entire landscape—we Galvestonians will have to get used to a major "missing tooth" along the Seawall. And then, of course, there's the nostalgia factor, that "oh, if those walls could only talk" feeling.

You wonder what stories, what memories, what images of the Isle in its heyday are now lost forever, carted away dumptruck-load by dumptruck-load over a few weeks.

But if it indeed had to go, dynamite was the kindest way to do the job.

There's just no sadder sight than to watch a stately old building die a slow and ignoble death under the wrecker's ball.

About twenty years ago, they tore down the Lovenberg Junior

High School, also on Seawall. I had to drive by the grim spectacle every day, and I watched in melancholy fascination as the demolition peeled away the old, Art Deco–style school's structure like the layers of an onion.

Day by day by agonizing day, the relentlessly pounding steel ball would strip away more and more of Lovenberg's dignity, opening up hallways and classrooms to wind, rain, and curious passersby. Here, a blackboard on a second-story wall still presided over its vanished classroom; in another room, opened up like a sardine can by the wreckers, a light fixture dangled crazily from the ceiling, and a clock still managed to cling to the wall, hanging by a single wire.

As the facade was slowly stripped away, the gym and the auditorium stood naked—their identities proclaimed to all by the words "Gymnasium" and "Auditorium," painted in 1933 WPA Deco script high on their walls.

It seemed like it took forever for Lovenberg School to come down—it was winter, and it rained a lot, making the sight of cockbilled Venetian blinds slowly slap-slapping in the breeze at a shattered window all the more pitiful.

Each day, as the wreckers ripped deeper and deeper into the school—as space after space was violated, I swear I could sense the ghosts fleeing the premises—ghosts of locker doors slamming, echoes of feet scampering down hallways just as the tardy bell rang, shades of daydreaming eyes gazing out at a shrimper on the Gulf instead of the long-division problem on the blackboard.

And finally, it was gone—hauled away, scraped clean, just a vacant lot devoid of ghosts or echoes or even a memory of the molar that had been rooted in that particular socket for fifty-seven years. Just a gap, a void, nothing more than nothing. So it will soon be with the old Buccaneer—a park will take its place—but at least it came down all at once, taking center stage at the very end, holding its head high to the last.

Today, Tomorrow, and Always

With Dreams of the Future in Our Heads

Heralding the arrival of the twenty-first century on Galveston Island was a never-to-be-forgotten occasion. We recalled the many events and changes that had taken place during the last 100 years, factored in the fantastic pace with which we advanced technology during the twentieth century, and tried to imagine what our Island would be like in 100 years, when we would gather to celebrate the year 2100 . . .

As we float in a crystal-clear sky in our personal Star-Tricraft (a recently developed vehicle that flies through the air, hovers over the water, or glides along the roadways, guided by a computer-chip "autodriver"), we see below us what appears to be a wondrous green water lily floating in the Gulf of Mexico. Slowly drifting downward, we are astounded by the beauty of this lush semi-tropical island and the changes that have taken place.

The Gulf waves lap at white, sandy beaches 150 feet wide, stretching the entire length of the Island (two islands, actually; fishermen eagerly flock to Sweetwater Pass, created by the Category 5 Hurricane Carlota in 2023 where 7½ Mile Road used to be—its boardwalk and restaurants are a bustling tourist destination).

The beaches slope gently from the surf line to meet a grand boulevard of inviting walkways. A gallery of public monuments now joins the venerable frolicking dolphins at the 45th Street Park. Facing the Gulf, benches invite weary strollers to sit awhile, breathe in the fresh sea air, and drink in the magnificent ocean vista. Rows of sheltering trees shade this pedestrian-only promenade. Gentle illumination casts a soft glow on nighttime strollers. Stretching from the tree line, cool, green, grassy terraces gently climb to a level of luxuriant tropical plants and multi-hued oleanders accented with a variety of palms. Nestled and almost hidden by the foliage are homes, hotels, lodges, resorts, restaurants, and shopping areas.

Obviating the need for the old Seawall, the new laser-regulated weather control protects the beaches by adjusting wave action. Amazingly, this weather-control system also masters storms and hurricanes, sometimes directing them over open water, other times dispersing them altogether. This technological marvel can also produce rain anywhere and anytime it is needed.

As we drift across the Island to the Bolivar Roads shore on the East End, we find a picturesque waterfront home development with a 2,000-slip marina, the largest of its kind in the Gulf.

Skimming over Galveston Harbor, we watch a hard-working port as huge commercial vessels load and unload, day and night. Right in the heart of the port, running parallel to the working docks, is a wide boardwalk with open squares sporting umbrella-shaded tables and lined with gift shops and eateries. At the cruise terminal, several vessels depart each day for exciting foreign ports of call.

Now, moving over the center of the Island City, we notice that the last of the old-fashioned power lines are gone, save those preserved at the county museum. In the laser age, all power and communications are sent directly without any demand for poles and wires. The Strand has changed little at street level, although now almost all the upper floors of the buildings are residential apartments and lofts. Postoffice Street is jammed with art galleries and boutiques, and most of the people who work there also live there. The Strand–Postoffice renaissance has spilled over onto other nearby blocks, and quaint shops, cafes, and coffee houses fill the Historic District. The sounds of music fill the downtown air as street musicians and band concerts continue a 250-year-old Isle tradition.

The Victorian homes in the East End look the same, but they have been skillfully updated to take advantage of twenty-first-century amenities while preserving their nineteenth-century

Sea, sand, and shells . . . some things never change.
—Robert John Mihovil

heritage. Most homes, old and new, provide storage for six multi-medium vehicles, usually three on the rooftop and three at ground level. In the kitchens, refrigerators and pantries automatically reorder groceries as they are used, and in each bathroom is a medical cubicle that scans the body and transmits a health report to the doctor. All homes have an electronic communications room where business is conducted by the adults, and children receive a quality formal education. All children are also assigned to a multi-educational circle, where they participate in group activities. In this setting, they take field trips and participate in sports, gardening, art, music, and many other enriching pursuits.

There are major changes at Galveston Intergalactic Airport. At this gateway to the Gulf, one can climb aboard a rocket plane and be launched into space for a thirty-minute trip to London, or catch a hovercraft to the Spaceport in the Gulf of Mexico to board a space cruiser for a tour of outer space, followed by a vacation on an orbiting resort that provides a truly "out-of-this-world" experience. We can still travel by land, too—we simply set our Star-Tricraft computer for our destination and computer chips embedded in the road will take over the driving while we enjoy the scenery and conversation. If our route takes us over water, our "Star" will hover gently and swiftly to our final destination. Of course, we can stop anywhere along the way—if we tell the computer navigator of our plans.

Still, some things never change . . . an early-morning fishing expedition when the only sounds are the cries of the birds in the distance and the soft splash of a jumping mullet . . . an afternoon sail on a glittering, sun-drenched sea . . . walking along the beach at sunset, marveling at the clear sky and deep colors, almost too lovely to look at. Here beats the true heart of Galveston, and hugged by the beach and the harbor, we are forever cradled in the watery embrace of Gulf and bay.

And So, to Bed

AN ESSAY BY MAX RIZLEY, JR.

Eventide—Where would we be without life's little rituals?

The morning walk, the daily soap opera, that midafternoon cup of coffee over at the mall, a weekly dinner with a friend—they are the thumbtacks that anchor the fabric of life.

You're just in time to share a favorite such ritual of mine—something I call "Watching the Beacon," a title that is only peripherally applicable. But here, pull up a chair, and I'll explain.

As you can see, we are seated on the balcony of my apartment, which overlooks a wide sweep of Offatt's Bayou here on the Island.

Across Offatt's is Scholes Field, and every evening, 'long about sundown, the green-and-white airfield beacon glimmers to life.

And that's what "Watching the Beacon" is—we sit here in the gathering dusk and look across the placid bayou at the airport terminal, waiting for the beacon to switch on.

Of course, "Watching the Beacon" has very little to do with it—that's just the excuse, the justification, for pulling a lawn chair out on the balcony every evening and doing absolutely nothing for an hour or so.

I love this time of day, don't you? The tail end of a blastingly hot September day—still hot, but a good-natured, after-hours kind of hot, not the vengeful furnace of a couple of hours before. The sun is hanging fat and red over Tiki Island; soon it will drop below the horizon, its rays caressing the hard-sculpted anvil of a dying thunderstorm with gentle pinks and oranges and crimsons.

It's quiet. The day's rat race is run, and a weary world now pauses to catch its breath. On the bayou, a little bay shrimper motors homeward with a muted purr, his gentle wake barely rippling the mirror-smooth water. A mullet flap-slaps the water, somewhere out there, and a sea bird rasps and creaks overhead, calling to his mate as he returns to his nest; then the silence descends like a mantle.

Now the lights are coming on. One by one, streetlights begin to shiver and dance in the heat waves over by the airport terminal, and a single red light pulses over on the tarmac where a helicopter has just come in from the day's last run.

On the bayou's far shore, a solitary yellow-white glimmer marks where some night fisherman has fired up his lantern, and away over there, all the way on the other side of the airport, the firefly headlights creep along the top of the Seawall.

And suddenly—right in front of us, just offshore—a sailboat, one of those big, lovely canoe-hull jobs, has glided silently out from behind our building. Gracefully, silently, it cleaves the still water; a woman's mirthful laugh filters up to us. At the stern, a flame flickers briefly in a stainless-steel kettle, and our noses savor for a moment the heady scent of steaks barbecuing.

Hmm. Getting darker now. A toy-like whirr and a fast-moving red light are all that tell us that one last fishing skiff is calling it a day, and the funky, organic, photosynthetic odor of full night settles in like a seductive incense as the stars begin their nightly journey. Antares glows, a baleful red eye in the southern sky, and right overhead, the Summer Triangle of Vega, Altair, and Deneb wheels through eternal space.

Back across Offatt's—ah! There it is! The airport beacon has begun its tireless nightly march. White . . . green . . . white . . . green. "Watch below, lay below," so the sailors say; time to close out another day.

And so, to bed.

Sundown . . . and the Scholes Field beacon glimmers to life and silently flashes as it keeps a nightly watch over the Island.

— Fletcher Harris

More Lore, Historical Resources

Books

Alperin, Lynn M. *Custodians of the Coast*. Galveston, Texas: U.S. Army Corps of Engineers Galveston District, 1977.

Cartwright, Gary. *Galveston: A History of the Island*. New York: Athenium Press, 1971. Dallas, Texas: TCU Press, 1998 (with Epilogue).

Christensen, Roberta Marie. *Pioneers of West Galveston Island*. Austin, Texas; Nortex Press, 1992.

Daniels, A. Pat. *A Fascinating Voyage on the Bolivar Ferry*. Crystal Beach: Peninsula Press of Texas, 1985, 1992.

———. *Gulf Coast Peninsula*. Crystal Beach: Peninsula Press of Texas, 1985.

Fornell, Earl Wesley. *The Galveston Era*. Austin: University of Texas Press, 1961.

Green, Nathan. *Story of the Galveston Hurricane and Story of the Galveston Flood*. Baltimore: R.H. Woodward Co., 1900. Gretna, Louisiana: Pelican Press, 2000.

Halstead, Murat. *The Horrors of a Stricken City*. American Pulishers Association: 1900. Gretna, Louisiana: Pelican Press, 2000.

Harper, Jack and John Newbern. *Odd Texas*. Dallas, Texas: Banks Upshaw & Co., 1936.

Hull, Pinky. *From Tent Show to Opera*. Crystal Beach, Texas: Peninsula Press of Texas, 1992.

Hyman, Harold M. *Oleander Odyssey*. College Station, Texas: Texas A&M University Press, 1990.

Kempner, I. H. *Recalled Recollections*. Dallas, Texas: The Eagan Co., 1961, 1981.

Kempner, Mr. and Mrs. Harris. *Letters From Sandy*. Lunenberg, Vermont: The Steinhouse Press, 1967.

Lewis, Carroll. *The Treasures of Galveston Bay.* Waco, Texas: Texian Press, 1977.

Lindbergh, Charles A. *The Wartime Journals of Charles A. Lindbergh.* New York: Harcourt, Brace, Jovanovich, 1970.

McComb, David G. *Galveston: A History.* Austin: University of Texas Press, 1961.

Miller, Ray. *Ray Miller's Galveston.* Austin: Capital Printing, 1983, 1984.

Newbitt, Robert. *Bob's Reader.* Galveston, Texas: Privately published, 1985.

Sharf, J. Thomas. *History of the Confederate States Navy.* New York: The Fairfax Press, 1866.

de Vaca, Cabeza. *Relaciones.* Zamora, Spain, 1542; Peabody Museum, Harvard University.

Wells, Tom Henderson. *Commodore Moore and The Texas Navy.* Austin: University of Texas Press, 1960, 1988.

Wiggins, Melanie: *They Made Their Own Laws.* Houston, Texas: Rice University Press, 1990.

———. *Torpedoes In The Gulf: Galveston And The U-Boats 1942–1943.* College Station: Texas A&M University Press, 1995.

———. *U-Boat Adventures: Firsthand Accounts from World War II.* Annapolis, Maryland: U.S. Naval Institute Press, 1999.

Works Progress Administration. "Texas, American Guide Series." New York: Hastings House, 1940.

PERIODICALS

The Galveston County Daily News, Galveston, Texas.
The Houston Chronicle, Houston, Texas.
The Houston Post, Houston, Texas.
The Dallas Morning News, Dallas, Texas.
InBetween Magazine, Galveston, Texas.
Islander/Bay Area Press, Galveston, Texas.